WITH

SUGAR 'N SPICE

WITH

SUGAR 'N SPICE

by

Daryl V. Hoole
Donette V. Ockey

Illustrations by Aurelia P. Richards

Published by
Deseret Book Company
Salt Lake City, Utah
1966
Articles from *The Improvement Era* used by permission.

Contents

Introduction

With the sweetness of sugar and the liveliness of spice,
Childrens' appetites for learning you'll successfully entice.
As you teach them gospel doctrines, you'll fill them with delight,
And eagerly they'll learn to do the things they know are right.
Home evenings can be special for such a little price—
Just a sprinkling of sugar and a little dash of spice!

The leaders of the Church have brought vividly to our attention that systematic and effective teaching of the gospel in the home is the need of the hour. They have given us inspired materials with which to work. The challenge to us as parents is to present this to our children in a way that will be appealing to them.

The subsequent chapters in this book will suggest some "Sugar 'n Spice" which you may use to help your children take an interest in the gospel teachings you are presenting to them.

In our Family Home Evenings, we have discovered two great truths: One is: *The better prepared we are as parents, the better our children behave.* The other one is: *The more creative and interesting is our approach to the lesson, the more the children learn and the longer they remember it.*

Preparation

Charles Schwab, the multimillionaire Bethlehem Steel man, accredits one simple principle for most of his success. One day he asked an efficiency expert, Ivy Lee: "If you can give us something to pep us up to do the things we know we ought to do, I'll gladly pay you anything within reason you ask."

"Fine," answered Mr. Lee, "I can give you something in 20 minutes that will step up your 'doing' by at least 50 per cent."

"All right," said Mr. Schwab, "let's have it."

Ivy Lee handed Charles Schwab a blank sheet of note paper and said: "Write down the six most important tasks you have to do tomorrow and number them in the order of their importance.

Now, put this paper in your pocket and the first thing tomorrow morning look at item number one and start working on it until it is finished. Then tackle item two in the same way; then item three; and so on. Do this until quitting time.

"Don't be concerned if you have only finished one or two. You'll be working on the most important ones. The others can wait. If you can't finish them all by this method, you couldn't have with any other method, either; and without some system, you'd probably not even have decided which was the most important.

"Do this every working day. After you've convinced yourself of the value of this system, have your men try it. Try it as long as you wish and then send me a check for what you think it is worth."

A few weeks later, Charles Schwab sent Ivy Lee a check for $25,000 with a letter saying the lesson was the most profitable he had ever learned.

This system made Charles Schwab one of the world's wealthy men. This same system can provide you with a wealth of spiritual blessings which will make you and your family rich for all eternity.

With the many, many cares of daily living, there just won't be time to prepare for a Family Home Evening unless you plan for the time, work for the time, and then take the time. When work and activities are planned in advance and then approached systematically, twice as much can be done in half the length of time. *There will be time to prepare and hold family home evenings if you plan.* Designate one day early in the week to prepare for your Family Home Evenings, and then make it number one on your list of activities. Set aside another day to hold your Family Home Evenings. Put this at the head of the list so that no matter what else happens, your Family Home Evening will take place. Nothing else really matters. President McKay often says, "No other success can compensate for failure in the home."

In our families we have found it most helpful to have a Family Home Evening notebook. It's just a simple looseleaf binder containing a pad of paper. We mothers prepare the program for a particular Family Home Evening (sometimes the children help

make the plans, too), write it down in the notebook, and then give it to our husbands so they can be ready to conduct the program. A pre-planned program in this manner eliminates the family's discussing "what song should we sing?" or "who wants to say the prayer?" which invariably ends in an unnecessary discussion. The children respect the plans in the notebook and their father's authority as patriarch of our family and head of our home. Frequently we write down the words to the songs to be sung. This helps our husbands join in the singing of Junior Sunday School hymns and Primary songs!

A typical program for our young children could be as follows: (A similar program, though on a more mature level, could be used for older children.)

Welcome: (parent or child)
Opening song: Jesus Wants Me for a Sunbeam (led by child)
Prayer: (child)
Family council: (conducted by father and should last five to ten minutes) brief discussion about activities and responsibilities of family members. This should be a pleasant time; not a battle-

ground! It's a good opportunity for a project or learning experience, such as teaching children how to answer the telephone correctly, how to make an introduction, what our address and telephone number are.
Poem: (led by child)
Songs: (led by child)
Story or recitation: (led by child)
Finger Play or Rest Exercise: (conducted by youngest child)
Language Lesson: (if either parent speaks a foreign language, this is a good time to teach a few words to the children. Children find it fun and easy to learn at a young age.)
Lesson: (mother or father)   Family Home Evening Manual
Activity: Family Home Evening Manual
Closing song: (led by child)   I Am a Child of God
Prayer: (family prayer with everyone taking a turn)
Refreshments:

A nineteen-year-old navy man was knocked off the deck of the carrier *Saratoga* by a jet plane blast. The sailor, who didn't know how to swim, fell 80 feet into the Atlantic Ocean. He immediately "learned to swim" and managed to stay in the water 90 minutes until he was rescued.

A Kansas farmhouse caught fire at midnight and sent five members of the family scurrying into the front yard. The sixth, a seventy-year-old grandfather who had suffered for years from rheumatism, was sleeping in the third-floor attic. He opened the window and climbed out on the roof. Watchers below screamed, "Don't jump!" He didn't. Instead, he stepped lightly onto a sagging telephone cable. Balancing effortlessly, he ran 30 feet along the swaying slack wire to a wooden roadside pole and climbed safely down to the ground.

Both the sailor and the elderly grandfather put forth their every effort to save themselves. They had to. Their lives were at stake.

It isn't easy to prepare gospel lessons and teach them to your children effectively. A great deal of effort is required to do so. But you have to. Your children's lives—their eternal lives—are at stake. Surely we will follow the council of our living prophet of the Lord and teach our children the gospel in the home.

It is sincerely hoped that the ideas in this book will suggest to you some "Sugar 'n Spice" which will be of help to you in conducting family home evenings and in teaching your children the gospel of Jesus Christ.

I
Retold Stories

The story is told of a great king and queen who lived long, long ago. One day a little prince was born to them, and the king gave a special feast and invited all the people of his kingdom to come so that they might rejoice together.

The great and wealthy men brought costly gifts to the little babe, with the exception of one young and very wise man. He came empty handed. However, he said to the king, "Your son has received many costly gifts. I will give him something more precious than jewels and gold. Each day as he grows I will tell him a story that will make him wise and righteous."

Each day as the years went by this young man came to the palace. Each day he told the little boy a story. The child did become wise and righteous because what he learned through the stories helped determine the kind of man he became.

We parents have a gift to give our children which is more precious than jewels and gold. The greatest gift that we can give them is that of *teaching them how to live, teaching them to love and obey the Lord, and instilling in their hearts a testimony of the gospel of Jesus Christ.*

A retold story is often much more effective in influencing children (grown-ups, too, for that matter) than generalizing, preaching, or lecturing. The greatest teacher of all, Jesus Christ, taught his people through stories, using the terminology and illustrations which were familiar to them. These parables are classic examples of excellent teaching.

Good stories, well told, are a vital part of successful Family Home Evenings. In many cases they offer just the "Sugar 'n Spice" needed to make a lesson long remembered, stimulating and motivating.

The many choice, well-developed stories in the *Church Family Home Evening Manual* offer a wonderful aid to us in teaching our children. Wise, conscientious parents are constantly alert to story ideas from other sources, too, which can meet various needs with their children and help these children grow up to be wise and righteous.

Build Character

An edifying story can help to build children's characters and make them better people. Strength in overcoming weaknesses and faults can be gained through stories, as you can see in this one adapted from the one our grandmother told us as children:

Gertie the Grumbler

Gertie was a lovely little girl who had pretty dark curls and blue eyes. She was learning to play the piano well, and she was a good student at school. Gertie was lovely, except for one terrible habit. She was a groaner and complainer. No matter what happened or what she did, there was always some reason why Gertie couldn't be happy or pleased. It seemed to her family that she grumbled constantly. That's why her mother and father and older brother called her Gertie the Grumbler.

The time came that Gertie was to turn nine years old. In an attempt to make Gertie happy, her mother had told her she could have a birthday party. It was Gertie's privilege to invite just as many friends as she wanted. She also chose the games and activities, the flavor of ice cream, and the decorations for the cake. Her parents even let her select a new dress to wear to the party. Everything was done to please Gertie and make her happy.

Gertie's young friends had a delightful time at the party. It had been a grand success—at least so Gertie's parents thought. But when it was all over, Gertie wasn't happy. She was sorry she had invited Ann. If she had invited Betty instead, Betty might have given her the pen and pencil set. Ann's gift was a book she had already read. Gertie complained so about her own decision of having chosen to take her friends to the zoo instead of a show. How she wished they had gone to the matinee instead. She grumbled about the refreshments. Strawberry ice cream is so common; she should have chosen the peppermint after all. Her new dress didn't suit her, she said. She wished she had taken the blue sailor style rather than this one.

That's how it always was. No matter what Gertie's family, friends, and teachers did to make her happy, Gertie found a reason to grumble. It wasn't long before Gertie didn't have any friends. Her teachers would shake their heads and say, "Gertie could be such a lovely, sweet girl if she just didn't grumble so much." Gertie's parents tried and tried to help her see this problem, but Gertie went right on grumbling.

A few years later when Gertie was a teenager, her older brother went away to school. Gertie loved her brother very much and decided to prepare a special box to send him for his birthday. She spent days baking his favorite cookies and wrapping them to be mailed. She took the baby-sitting money she had earned the past few weeks and bought him a beautiful sport sweater—the kind he said he would like to have. There was even enough money left over to buy him a pair of socks to match the sweater. She included two magazines he liked to read as an extra surprise. After the box was mailed, she could hardly wait to receive his thank-you letter. She waited and waited, but no letter came.

When her brother returned home for Christmas vacation, Gertie asked first thing about the birthday box she had sent. "Oh," he said, "I got it all right, but by the time I shared the cookies with my roommates there weren't many left for me. I wish the sweater had been green instead of blue. That's the color all the fellows are wearing this season. And next time you send me something, remember I like stretch socks better than the ones you bought. The dormitory lounge is full of reading material if I should ever have any time after studying, so don't bother about magazines any more."

By this time Gertie was in tears. How could her brother be so ungrateful, so unappreciative of all she had done? How could he be such a grumbler and complainer? Then Gertie saw it all. Her brother was merely treating her as she had treated him and everyone else all her life. Suddenly she realized what a terrible grumbler she had been. She had let the bad habit of complaining and finding fault with things take over her life and spoil her personality.

The day her brother taught her this valuable lesson marked the turning point in Gertie's life. From that time on she looked for the best in everything that happened. It was really hard at first. Grumbling had become such a habit with Gertie that she found herself grumbling without even realizing it. Each time she caught herself even thinking about it, she would try harder to put a happy thought in her mind in its place. It became her dream to become known as Gertie the Gracious One or Gertie the Grateful One. And before long she was!

Move to Laughter or Tears

Stories can inspire and touch children emotionally and cause them to respond with more grateful hearts, more generous natures, and a rededication to things in life which are most precious and important.

Joey

The store windows were just as magnificent as they had been last week, but Joey stared unseeingly into them. He didn't notice the electric train that he had admired for over a half hour; and he didn't even laugh when the toy conductor hopped on and off at each station. Joey was thinking about last night.

In all his nine years, he had never had to make such an important decision. When he had come home from school, he noticed that his mother, who was usually cheerful, looked worried. After dinner, Joey's mother had said, "Joey, you help Connie get to bed, will you, please?"

"Of course," Joey had replied. "What story are you going to read us tonight?"

"None, tonight, dear," his mother had said, and Joey was too surprised to protest. He could not remember one single night that his mother had not read them a story or poem. Connie had gone quietly to bed because she, too, was confused. After Joey had listened to his little sister's simple prayer, he returned to the kitchen."

"Joey," his mother said then, "I want to talk to you." They both sat down at the kitchen table. "It's about Rags. Rags is a good little dog and never causes any trouble at all, but it still costs money to feed him." Joey kept his eyes down. He was afraid of what was coming. "You need a new winter coat badly this year, and yesterday when I priced them they were more expensive than I had counted on. I'm sorry, Joey, but if we keep Rags, you can't have a winter coat this year."

Joey knew that he needed the winter coat. His old one was so terribly small it looked silly on him and was so worn out and torn that it didn't begin to keep the cold out. But Joey also needed Rags. He looked at the little dog lying by the cold hearth. He knew that Connie played with the dog all day while Joey was at school. What would she do without Rags? But, what would he do without a winter coat? His mother continued. "I love Rags as much as you do, Joey. The decision is yours."

Joey thought. "Can I tell you in the morning?"

"Of course," his mother had said. Joey knew that his mother realized how he loved the little dog he had found three years ago. She gave him a hug and a kiss, and he had run off to bed. But he did not sleep. He had cried and cried and cried all night long because he knew what the decision must be. His eyes were red and swollen when he told his Mother that he would take Rags to town after school and give him away to somebody. His mother had tried to smile. "Some other family can probably give him better food and a warmer place to sleep than we can anyway." Joey knew this was true.

A sudden bark reminded Joey that he was downtown with Rags in his arms. He had been there an hour and his feet and hands were ice-cold. He gave Rags a squeeze and touched his lips to Rags' ear. He started slowly up the street. People couldn't help noticing the tiny figure who was so thinly clad and carrying a dog. Nor could they overlook the expression of complete unhappiness that was on his face. While passing the pet store Joey heard a little boy say, "Oh, Mother, I'm going to ask Santa to bring me that little spotted puppy." Joey looked at the little boy. Then he looked at the lady beside him as she said, "But, Richard, Santa is already bringing you so many things that he hasn't room in his bag for a puppy dog." Joey took a deep breath and walked up to the boy. "You can have this dog." His name is Rags and . . . ." Joey almost choked as he finished his sentence . . . "and he's such a good dog." The boy laughed, and the mother smiled. "Rags is certainly a good name. I don't want that dog, Mother. He's too ugly!" Joey felt the tears burning his eyes. He turned and ran down the street. Rags was thin and scrawny, and his fur was dull and unbrushed, but that didn't matter to Joey. Joey loved the little dog.

Joey slushed through the snow, not knowing or caring where he was going. Rags snuggled up against him and helped to keep him warm. Suddenly Joey saw a Christmas tree in the window of a large brick house. The Christmas tree was just as pretty as the ones in the store windows. He walked up the path and peeked into the window. The lovely green boughs of the Christmas tree were decorated with ornaments of gay colors, and they spread over beautifully wrapped gifts. Joey looked at the smiling angel on top. "The people who live here certainly must be happy," thought Joey. "I'll bet they'd be good to Rags." He rang the door-bell, and after a moment's wait the door opened. Joey was silent. He had hardly been aware of what he was doing and when a lady appeared at the door, he had absolutely no idea of what to say or do. "Would you like this dog? His name is Rags," is what Joey finally blurted out. He could hear children fighting inside. The lady said, "What would we want with such a dog?" and shut the door.

Joey stood before the closed door, speechless. How could anyone with such a beautiful Christmas tree and nice house be so grouchy and impolite? Joey slowly walked down the path. Well, he was glad that they didn't want Rags. They seemed like such a grumpy family they probably wouldn't love Rags at all. Rags began to get restless and Joey decided that he had better hurry and give him to someone. It got a little bit harder each time. Resolutely he walked to the door of the next house. He could smell spicy cookies and he could hear gay music. "These people must be happy," he thought as he pushed the doorbell. This time a teenaged girl answered the door. "This is my dog, Rags," said Joey. "Would you take him? We can't keep him anymore." The girl smiled, but her reply was firm. "We really have no use for a dog." Just then a little girl streaked through the hall with a boy about Joey's age in pursuit. He gave the little girl a swat that sent her rolling on the floor, and screams followed. "My good-ness," thought Joey as the door closed, "these people can't be happy at all. If I treated Connie like that, we certainly wouldn't have any fun." He was glad that these people didn't want Rags either.

Joey went to the next house. A man came to the door, and when he heard what Joey wanted, he laughed. "Ella," he said to the lady in the next room, "this little boy wants to give us a dog."

"A what?" asked the lady, and then she began to laugh, too. The man slammed the door so hard it almost hit Joey in the face. He turned and ran and ran and ran. He slid twice in the snow, but was up again each time, still clutching Rags. He finally burst into his own little home and fell exhausted and sobbing in his Mother's arms. At the sight of Rags, Connie squealed with delight. The mother was wise enough not to question Joey at that time. She took his wet clothes off and put his warm pajamas on him. Then she gave him a bowl of steaming hot porridge. Still sobbing, Joey said, "Nobody loved Rags, Mother. All the people have pretty Christmas trees and many presents and good food to eat and nice houses to live in, and they all have warm winter coats, but none of them are happy. They could probably give Rags better food, but we love him. Don't make me give him away, Mother, please don't. I can go without a winter coat."

On Christmas morning while Mother read them the Christmas story from the Bible, Connie and Joey sat in their cold little house with Rags between them. As Joey heard the humble story of the birth of Christ, he knew that pretty Christmas trees or presents or expensive food or nice homes didn't make people happy. It was love. And then Joey knew that they were the happiest family in the city: Mother, Joey, Connie, and Rags.

Create Good Feelings and Happiness

Not only are stories an effective teaching medium, but they can set the stage for better feelings and happiness in families so that the Spirit of the Lord can dwell in the home and so that lessons can be taught.

A lovely young mother told me about her grandmother who had eleven children and managed so well that they grew up in a happy, harmonious home. The young mother wondered what the secret was. She learned that it happened like this in Grandmother's home:

One day the sons who were supposed to be sawing wood were quarreling. The mother was hurrying to prepare a dinner for church officials, but she stopped and went out and sat on a block of wood near where the boys were sawing, and said the magic words: "Let me tell you a story." Soon thereafter the mother and sons were laughing together. Later when the mother went inside, the boys resumed their work without any thought of what they had been quarreling about.

This mother, now a grandmother, took the time to create the happiness and harmony which were in her home. How magic the words can be: "Let me tell you a story. . . ."

Cause a Behavioral Change

It's a tremendously challenging experience to raise a family, and parents are often perplexed by problems and wonder just how to handle them. Stories, either original ones created by the parents or those gleaned from other sources, can frequently meet a need and help solve a family problem. Bad language, telling falsehoods, taking things which don't belong to one, unwillingness to work, sassiness, and untidiness are some of the typical problems which appropriate stories can help correct. Following are two sample stories which we have repeated many times in our home to help them become part of one of our children's lives.

The Story of Three Families

Once upon a time there were three families that lived next door to one another in houses just alike. Not only were their houses alike, but the families themselves were alike—except for one thing. In each family there were a father, a mother, a girl, a boy, and a baby. The fathers all went to work early each morning. The mothers all stayed home during the day to clean, cook, sew, iron, and tend the children. The children went to the same school, and the babies played together. Now, I suppose you're wondering what it was that made these families different.

One family was called the Charles Clutter family, the second was the Carl Careless family, and the third was the Timothy Tidy family. Now do you know what made these families different from each other?

The Charles Clutter family lived in a pretty house. At least it was pretty when they first moved into it. But whenever the children came home from school, they would just throw their coats hats, and mittens on the nearest chair—and sometimes these articles even landed on the floor. They put their schoolbooks down wherever they happened to be, and often the baby got into the papers and scattered and tore them. If they went to the kitchen for a snack, they left the milk on the table (where it got sour and had to be thrown away) and the cracker box open on the cupboard. They set the dirty glasses on the drainboard, or sometimes they even carried their snack into their rooms and left the empty glass in there. Whenever they played games, they left them out until pretty soon the parts were lost or ruined. When getting ready for bed at night, they dropped their clothes wherever they happened to be, and pretty soon they didn't have any clean clothes to put on—and those that were clean were wrinkled and needed ironing—and even if some were both clean and pressed, they couldn't find them in all that clutter anyway. The baby's toys were scattered all over and so he seldom played with them because he couldn't ever find what he wanted. One time Mr. Clutter even broke his ankle because he stepped on some toys on the stairway and fell.

The worst part of the story is that Mr. and Mrs. Clutter were no better than their children. Mr. Clutter always dropped his briefcase anywhere he chose when he came home from work and threw his hat on the living-room couch (where somebody sat on it and ruined it). He laid his tools down all over the house, and pretty soon it was so hard to find them again that he didn't fix the broken screen or the leaky faucet or the broken toys.

Mrs. Clutter left her sewing all over and misplaced the dishes and the groceries and the clean clothes. If a button came off anything, it always got lost until all the clothes were pinned instead of buttoned. And sometimes they couldn't even find a pin, and then they did look awful! She seldom did the housework because it was too much bother to pick up everything so she could vacuum or dust or sweep. She had a terrible time when shopping because she didn't know whether they were really out of things at home or whether she just couldn't find them. One time she left some medicine where it shouldn't be, and the baby ate it. Then they had to take him to the hospital.

Well, you can imagine what kind of family this turned out to be. They were always so busy looking for things that they didn't have time for any fun. And they were all unhappy and angry all the time and the children never brought their friends home to their cluttered house. They were embarrassed when-

ever anyone came because the house was such a mess. And
pretty soon their house looked like this:

and they looked like this:
The Carl Careless family was just like the Charles Clutter
family except that Mrs. Careless really did care about keeping
everything orderly. So she spent all day long following the rest
of the family around and picking up after them. Of course she
kept telling the rest of the family that they should be more careful, and sometimes she'd even yell at them to try and make
them be more orderly. She was always tired and cranky from
doing so much work that she never had time to do the things
she really wanted to do. The children didn't like to be told the
same thing over and over again, and so they didn't spend any
more time at home than they had to. Even Mr. Careless didn't
like coming home after work to a wife that was so tired and cross
all the time. So even though their house looked like this:

they looked like this:

The third family, the Timothy Tidy family, was entirely different from the Careless and Clutter families. When the children came home from school, they found it was just as easy to hang up their wraps neatly on hooks in their closets. And they put their books on a special shelf in their rooms where the baby couldn't get into them. Their mother didn't mind if they had a snack because they always cleaned up afterwards. When they wanted to play a game, they knew just where to find it, and they enjoyed the same games for many years because the pieces were never lost or broken. It only took them a few minutes to get ready for school in the mornings because their clothes were always clean and pressed and hanging in their closets. Mr. Tidy never left his briefcase and hat where they could be ruined or misplaced, and he kept his tools in a special place so he could always find them. Mrs. Tidy kept the house shining clean and never left anything out where the baby could get into it. She only had to spend a few hours a day doing the housework, and then she could spend the rest of her time doing special things for her family. Best of all, she was always cheerful and happy, and her children and husband loved to be at home with her. The children were always proud to bring their friends home, and when the doorbell rang, they could enjoy having company come without being embarrassed. And the funny part is that it took the Tidy family so much less time to be Tidy than it took the Clutter and Careless families to be cluttered and careless. And the Tidy family's house always looked like this:

and they looked like this.

Which family should we be like?

Project Tidiness: Give each family member 25 beans in a little bag or jar. During the week, whenever someone of the family finds an object out of place, he picks it up and "sells" it back to the person it belongs to for one bean. At the end of the week, the one having the most beans gets a special treat or reward. Since tidiness is more habit than anything else, this game could be continued until the tidiness habit is solidly formed among all family members.

Three Is a Crowd

Carol, Barbara, and Sally were three little girls who lived on the same block in the same neighborhood. They were the same age and attended the same Sunday School and Primary classes. They were all in the second grade at school. They were lovely little girls and everyone liked them. They had one difficult problem, however. For some reason it is often very hard for three people to get along well. Two children can be good friends and so can four children; but when three try to play together, it seems that one is often left out. One day Barbara and Sally would be very friendly and leave Carol alone. Another day, Carol and Sally would play together and call out rude, thoughtless things to Barbara. Sometimes Barbara would feel that Carol was her very best friend and invite her to go sledding, leaving Sally home with hurt feelings. Then there were times when all three would do something together, but after an hour or so two of them would pair off and leave the third little girl out of the fun and plans.

Sally's mother observed all this and felt very sorry each time it was Sally's turn to be "out." She wondered what to do. She knew that a social rule says, "Three is a crowd," and there isn't much hope in changing that. She realized that trying to force the girls to be friendly toward one another all the time would only create more problems. Using forms of bribery to draw one of the girls to play with her daughter would be detrimental to everyone concerned. It wouldn't be wise to complain to the other mothers; it's better that mothers not become involved in children's neighborhood squabbles! The only thing to do was to work with Sally in handling the problem in a mature way.

She helped Sally understand that it is a very difficult thing for three little girls to be friends. Someone is nearly always left out, and it does not necessarily mean that that particular little girl is any less desirable as a friend. Each one has to take a turn at being alone. Sally learned that there were three things she could do. One, when it was her turn to be friends with either Barbara or Carol, she should be careful not to say things about the other one which could hurt her in any way. Name-calling and making fun of someone else were not to be done. Her mother explained to her that whatever she does in life comes right back to her. If she said naughty things about Carol or Barbara, she could be certain they would say naughty things about her another day. This was a hard lesson for Sally to master because seven-year-old girls are still learning about things such as this. She slipped sometimes and did say some mean things, but then she would remember and try harder next time to "do unto others as you would be done by."

The second thing Sally could do was to make herself an even more delightful person to be around. She could be sweeter and more gracious and thoughtful. She could be fun loving and have suggestions and ideas for good times. It would help her to exert herself a little—put herself forward—and plan special occasions and projects in which she could include both girls. She should do *more* than her part to be a good friend.

The other thing to do was to develop other friends, too, so that at times when she was lonely she would invite a girl from another neighborhood to come and play. This helped Sally to be a better friend and have more ideas for fun when it was her day to be friends with Barbara or Carol. Also, Susan found that there are lovely little girls everywhere, and she appreciated the opportunity of having many friends.

Sally's mother explained that each year as the three girls became more grown up it would be easier for them to get along. The problems of selfishness and jealousy should disappear over the years. Sally learned to be thankful for this difficult, but beneficial, experience in learning to get along better with others.

Help Meet an Emotional Need
You Are a Jewel

Ella struggled to hold back her tears as she ran along the stone walk to Aunt Susan's apartment at the rear of her home. As Ella rushed up to her aunt, the tears, which had been too near the surface too much of the time lately, spilled over. "Oh, Aunt Susan," sobbed Ella, "nobody likes me. I'm just no good. I wish I weren't such a dumb. . . ." More sobs blotted out the rest of her words.

Ella always ran to Aunt Susan when she had problems. And what thirteen-year-old girl hasn't! Ella felt Aunt Susan understood her and somehow had a way of making her heart lighter again. Ella was grateful Aunt Susan had come to live in their apartment after Uncle Tim had passed away.

Aunt Susan had laid her knitting aside and was waiting for her young niece to go on with her problem. "Why do you feel that no one likes you? What makes you think you're dumb and no good?" she encouraged.

"It's just terrible, Aunt Susan, to live with Bevie and Ruth. They make me feel awful. Bevie is so friendly with everyone and can always find so much to talk about. Everybody just loves her. Almost every phone call at our house is for her. She gets invited to all the parties and has all the fun. Whenever I'm in a group of people, I either say the wrong thing or . . . or else I can't think of anything to say at all. Bevie isn't afraid to talk to anyone, and she's so clever and full of fun. Oh, I wish I could be like Bevie.

"And Ruth makes me feel so dumb and stupid. She can do anything. Mother and Daddy are forever bragging about her accomplishments. I never do anything worth mentioning. It seems all I hear around our house is talk about her scholarship from the university or how the new three-piece suit she just made is so beautiful or something else she has done. Even the bishop said the other day that when Ruth goes away to school he doesn't know what he'll do for a Sunday School organist. She's always in demand for her piano playing. Everyone says things like: "There's just no one quite like Ruth," or "She's the most talented and capable girl I've ever seen." It goes on and on, and the more she does, the dumber I feel."

Aunt Susan thought for a long time before responding to Ella. Finally she said, "I can understand how you feel, Ella. It would be difficult to live with two very popular, talented older sisters. It could make you feel quite inferior. I would like to make three suggestions to you. You might like to write them down and read them often—even memorize them— so that you'll remember them for the rest of your life.

"First, you're comparing yourself with someone else. This is unfair. You're much younger than your sisters. Bevie has had several years more practice talking with people and learning to express herself well and saying clever things. I feel sure you'll gain in confidence and will feel you have more to contribute to conversations as you grow older. Time has done a lot for Ruth, too. As I think back to her piano playing when she was your age, it sounded just the way yours does. Who's to say what accomplishments will be yours by the time you graduate from high school? You've been busy laying your foundation for life these past thirteen years. It's just about now that you can start to build on that foundation and really do things. It's all wrong to compare yourself with others, Ella. The only real basis for comparison is within yourself. Don't feel bad if your piano playing—or anything else—isn't as good as Ruth's. Just make certain that you play better now than you did a year ago. It's wonderful to have people such as Ruth inspire you to do better and reach loftier goals but compete with yourself— not someone else!

"Now the second thing I want you to remember always is this. That which someone else does, needn't detract from that which you do. Just because Bevie has lots of friends doesn't mean that you have any fewer friends of your own. Just because someone has beautiful eyes doesn't mean that your eyes are ugly. Nothing Ruth knows or does or has need detract from what you know or do or have.

"And third and most important, Ella, our Father in heaven has taken great care to create each one of us individually. Don't try to make yourself like someone else. Be grateful for your own talents and gifts and do your best to cultivate them. Why, it was just last week at Relief Society I heard several mothers discussing baby sitters. They mentioned your name and said how confident they feel when you are with their children and how much their children enjoy you. Sister Astin said that because of your conscientiousness toward responsibility and your ability to handle children exceptionally well you make an ideal baby sitter.

"I've heard your mother say on many occasions how she depends on you to help her. She says you always do your work well and willingly and do so much to make your home a better place to be.

"Have you ever realized, Ella, that when someone is ill, you know just what to do to bring the most comfort? I recall my bout with rheumatism last winter . . . it was you who took the time to run my errands, keep fresh flowers by my bedside, and cheer me through your visits. You have a fine mind, Ella. I've observed that you have a quest for knowledge. You love school and do very well there. I could go on, Ella, for you have many gifts and talents which make you special just the way you are. I read something last week I want to share with you. I hope it will impress you as it did me. Did you know that no two diamonds are, or ever have been, alike? This diamond I am wearing on my finger is unlike any other diamond on earth. That's one of the reasons the diamond has become, since ancient times, the gem of kings and emperors and holds the greatest value of all wordly possessions. No two diamonds are alike, but they are all jewels. Never forget that you are a jewel, Ella."

Ella's heart felt lighter than ever before as she skipped home along the stone path.

Inspire Faith

Stories—including experiences and examples—can inspire faith, help children develop an understanding of the gospel, and build testimonies in their hearts.

The Balloon Ride

One day, many, many years ago, an old-fashioned country fair was held. Families for miles around visited the fair. The balloon ride was the big attraction.

Jenny and her family were at the fair, and Jenny was excitedly sitting in the basket of the balloon, awaiting her family and other passengers. Suddenly a gust of wind blew the balloon's rope out of the attendant's hands. Up, up, up it went. The people, river, houses, trees and animals grew smaller and smaller and smaller as Jenny watched from the side of the basket.

Jenny was terribly frightened! In fact she was frantic! What should she do? How high would the balloon go? What was going to happen to her?

Then she knew what to do. Jenny prayed about it. She asked her Heavenly Father what she should do. Soon she noticed a rope and felt impressed to pull it. As she did so, some of the gas in the balloon was released and the balloon descended just a little. She pulled the rope again, and the balloon went down a little more. She pulled it again and again, each time letting a little more of the gas escape. She felt impressed to pull only a little bit at a time so that the balloon wouldn't go down too fast. As she went lower and lower, she looked over the edge of the basket and saw the people, river, houses, trees, and animals growing larger and larger again. She was almost to the ground! How thrilled and thankful she was.

She landed safely in a meadow not far from the country fair grounds. How happy everyone was to see her. How happy she was to see them! As she hugged her mother, she learned that her parents, too, had prayed. They were grateful to Heavenly Father who had heard and answered their prayers.

How fortunate are families where parents know the truth and the things which matter most in life. How blessed are families when parents effectively communicate this to their children. We have a divinely inspired program and materials with which to work. We who have been given much must remember that much is required. Let's take advantage of every opportunity to tell our children stories which can help them become wise and righteous. An incident which appeared in an issue of ZCMIRROR, employees' publication of ZCMI department store in Salt Lake City, will help us to understand how precious this privilege is:

The little boy's eyes fairly sparkled as he listened to the funny talking teddy bear introduce himself at the record center, and he laughed aloud as the bear continued to talk in his funny voice.

His parents smiled with approval, so the salesperson thought he might show them how clever the toy really is. The teddy bear is attached to a record player and has a speaker inside so little folk can believe he really speaks to them.

There are six teddy bear albums, and the records can be played on it, too.

The parents didn't seem to have much to say, but they appeared to be pleased with the toy. The mother then took a pad of paper from her handbag and hurriedly wrote a note to the salesman.

He wasn't so surprised—parents often have to be sly when they're doing their Christmas shopping with the young ones along. But this is what the note said:

"We want to get this teddy bear for our little boy. It is really an answer to our prayers. . . . You see, my husband and I are deaf and unable to speak. Now he will be able to hear the bedtime stories we've always wanted to tell him."

II

Family Activities

We remember 10% of what we read;
We remember 20% of what we see;
We remember 50% of what we read and see;
We remember 90% of what we do.

Our Father in heaven has said, ". . . this is my work and my glory—to bring to pass the immortality and eternal life of man." (Moses 1:39.) To accomplish this great purpose, he has placed us here on earth to let us work out our own salvation. He will do nothing for us that we can do for ourselves because he knows that our individual development and progress depend upon our experiencing and *doing* things for ourselves.

As earthly parents, we, too, are deeply concerned about the immortality and eternal life of our children. It is our sacred obligation to set the stage so that they might experience and do the things which will help bring about their eventual exaltation. In conducting weekly Family Home Evenings, the more children actually *do*, the more they will remember, and consequently the more they will be able to apply in their lives. An activity could well be just what you need to add "Sugar 'n Spice" to learning.

This chapter discusses some Family Home Evening activities which you may wish to adapt for your family.

Service Projects

Prepare, with lots of help from your children, lovely "take-out" dinners to send to a home where there is illness or some other emergency, or where a new baby has just arrived. An oven-fresh loaf of bread or other baked goods are a real treat to a family under any circumstances! Arrange to have your children do as much of the planning, preparing, and delivering as possible. A choice family in our city raises a lovely garden each year mainly so their children can share the flowers and vegetables.

At holiday time, such as Christmas, Valentine Day, and Easter, sharing projects can help children to think less about "what am I going to get" and a little more regarding "what can I give."

Service projects of any kind—from baby sitting to setting out a widow's garbage cans—can help children cultivate one of life's most important virtues and learn for themselves that it truly is more blessed to give than to receive.

Planning, Preparing, Taking Part

Family Home Evenings can be doubly effective if the children take turns actually planning and conducting them, under the direction of the father who should preside. Older children, who might be inclined toward boredom, could have tremendous experiences preparing and teaching some of the lessons. Not only does this alleviate the boredom, but it really develops these grown children because the teacher always learns the most!

Young children can recite poems, tell stories, and give short talks along with the regular weekly Family Home Evening lessons. Our young children love to present lessons which they have prepared all on their own. We are constantly amazed by their creative abilities as they use visual materials, "attention getters," and original stories. What these little lessons may lack in continuity sometimes is well compensated by what the children gain in real growth and development. One lesson given is worth several lessons heard!

Older children can be assigned book or article reviews from church or other worthwhile publications; for instance, a teen-ager could read the current issue of *The Improvement Era* or *The Instructor* and then report on the article which impressed him most.

Tremendous growth on the part of children can be realized by having them regularly give talks as a part of your Family Home Evening. Children may either select their own subjects or on occasion the parents might assign a subject to which they should speak.

Once in a while it can be challenging and worthwhile to call on a child for an impromptu talk. You might say, "Steve, will you please stand and talk to us for two minutes about the Word of Wisdom," or "Ann, would you please take several minutes to tell us what the ideal of temple marriage means to you," or "Beth, would you please give a short talk on the significance of prayer." Such an activity helps teach children to think on their feet, it helps parents to know how their children really feel, and certainly no one is ever bored!

Homemade Television Programs or Film Strips

A "television program" or "film strip" offers a unique family activity. Illustrations and a script, if desired, should be pasted on a roll of paper, and then the roll of paper is to be inserted in a pasteboard box so that it can be viewed by the audience of family members as it is rolled. Following is a sample script with illustrations:

A Special Little Penny

In the child's outstretched hand
The pennies waited eagerly,
Wondering what he'd do with them
And what their future tasks would be.
At first there were ten pennies,
Then suddenly just nine,
For the child had taken one and said
"Little penny, you're not mine.
You're a very special penny
With a special job to do.
You're the brightest, shiniest one of all

That's why I've chosen you.
Each time I get ten pennies
One must be returned
To my Heavenly Father to do his work,
For the law of tithing I have learned.
I have so many blessings
And such a grateful heart
And even though one cent is small
I'm glad to do my part.
So I'll put you in my tithing box

And you must patient be,
Till Sunday when I'll take you out
To go to church with me."
While the little penny waited,
He thought of his job with pride
And promised to do the best he could.
He felt happy and good inside.

Then Sunday came, and to church he went
Clutched in the child's hand
And was given to the bishop
Just as the child had planned.
But now the little penny
Was no longer all alone;
There were many others also

Sharing his new home.
Not only were there pennies
But nickels, dimes as well,
And many, many dollars—
Just how many he couldn't tell.
"What are you all doing here?"
The little penny asked;
"Are you ordinary money

Or do you, too, have a special task?"
Then an older, wiser, nickel said,
"We're special, just like you,
For we're all tithing money
With important jobs to do."
"I know that tithing money
Belongs unto the Lord,
And that those who pay their tithing
Will receive a rich reward.
But just exactly what's my job?
In what way can I work?
I want to know just what to do,

For I don't want to shirk."
"We'll tell you," said the others,
And they smiled at the penny,
"For there is much work to be done
And the helpers must be many.
Temples and chapels must be built
In which church members can meet.
So we must do whatever we can
To make this work complete.
The missionary program
Which brings eternal joy
Is helped by tithing pennies
From every girl and boy.
Seminaries, institutes,
And schools in foreign lands,
Are just another worthy cause
Where we must lend a hand.
There are still more places
Where we can be of service,
The wondrous genealogy
Is a program that deserves us.
At conference time and other times
Throughout the world we go
Bringing people inspiration
Through TV and radio.
The leaders of the Church
With much traveling to do
To visit Saints throughout the world
Need help from me and you.
Then there are many other things
In which we do a share,
You can see just how important
We are to people everywhere."
"My goodness," said the penny,
"I am so very small,
And there's so much work that should be done;
Am I any good at all?"
"Oh, yes," sang all the others.
"If we don't work as one,
We could never even start
On all that must be done.
That's why every single penny
Is as important as can be
In carrying out the work of God

To help build eternity."
So the shiny, happy penny
Was sent with the nickels and dimes
To the headquarters of the Church
To join others from all the climes.
Together they're working diligently
To fulfil a marvelous plan,
For tithing is part of the Lord's special way
To bring happiness and blessing to man.

Musical Evenings

Musical renditions on the part of family members can be coordinated with regular Family Home Evenings to the enjoyment and edification of everyone.

Singing together as a family is delightful and helps to establish an atmosphere of love and happiness. Our two-year-old daughter likes this time best of all because she "leads" the singing. This is one way even a very young child can learn to participate.

Dramatizations, Pantomimes, Charades

Simple dramatizations with the family members forming the cast can impress a lesson on the minds of children. A number of the stories in the *Church Family Home Evening Manual* could be adapted as dramatizations. Incidents from the Bible, Book of Mormon, or church history easily lend themselves to dramatizations.

Pantomimes are simple, yet they can be very effective. Each Christmas Eve at our traditional family get-together, our children along with their little cousins (all children are under six) pantomime the story of the First Christmas. The parts of Mary and Joseph are rotated among the children from year to year, and a favorite doll or a newborn baby plays the part of baby Jesus. Robes, scarves, and towels bedeck the other children out as the shepherds and wisemen. It seems that even the littlest shepherd is able to stand still while an older child reads the story of the First Christmas from the Gospel of Luke. Then everyone joins in singing "Away in a Manger."

Charades is a game whereby the audience attempts to guess a story or incident as the actors dramatize or depict in some way the meaning of each word in the title. Playing charades is another way to make a lesson memorable.

Memories Evening

To help build vivid memories and correct values in the minds of children of what things in life are most precious and important, a Memories Evening could be held occasionally. Family albums and record books could be enjoyed or family slides or movies could be viewed. New pictures might be taken. Tape recordings could be reviewed and perhaps a new tape could be made. Memories of special events connected with family trips and outings could be recalled. An additional highlight to the evening could be having each person present express what his choicest experience of the year has been.

Special Guests

A young boy received a bicycle for his sixth birthday. Before his parents gave him the bike, however, they invited a policeman friend (in full uniform) to visit one of their Family Home Evenings. He talked to the children about bicycle safety and other safety rules pertinent to them. These rules coming directly from this friendly policeman were much more impressive and helpful than anything parents could say.

A fireman could be invited in to talk about fire safety and how to work with matches and campfires.

Some children never have the privilege of seeing a returned missionary much closer than from where they sit in church to the pulpit. Lasting values could be gleaned by inviting an outstanding, enthusiastic returned missionary to your home to talk to your children. His spirit and enthusiasm could be a great motivating factor in helping a young child live worthy of a mission.

Family Fix-It Night

Projects can provide great times. A family "fix-it night" when the mother and girls mend and the father and sons handle any maintenance work and repair jobs is fun as well as helpful. This activity, as well as any other, should be crowned with a freezer of homemade ice cream, freshly popped corn, root beer floats, or some other treat.

Displays

Let the family show off their creative abilities. If you have a place in your home for a bulletin board, a table or mirror in the living room, or any other appropriate place, the children would love making different types of displays for these areas. They can use holiday or seasonal themes, or perhaps they can illustrate an important gospel teaching or something you are currently emphasizing in your Family Home Evenings. Turn them loose with crepe paper, construction paper, pictures, and all kinds of odds and ends. You might be surprised what they can come up with!

Buzz Sessions

It might be effective to hold occasional buzz sessions during your lessons or when discussing a family problem. Divide the family into at least two groups and allow them a few minutes to discuss the problem and exchange ideas. Then have one member from each group summarize the discussion and report to the entire family.

Question Box

QUESTION
BOX

A question box can take just part of the evening or occasionally take the entire lesson period. Let family members know in advance when you will be using the question box so they can put any questions they want in it. You may limit the questions to one particular subject or open it to questions in any category. Then the family may answer these questions together, assign just one member to answer, or even have a special visitor come in to answer questions some evening. The question box can also be used as a game by putting in questions regarding recent family night lessons or gospel subjects and letting family members take turns drawing questions and answering them.

What Are Families For?

Children need to learn early in life how they fit into their family and what is expected of them. Some children grow up feeling that their parents should be their slaves, doing anything and everything the child desires. Other children may grow up feeling they carry an unfair share of the family responsibility and fail to realize the many things their parents are doing in their behalf.

It is important to teach our children that each family member has responsibilities and contributions to make to the family and that even though each may contribute something entirely different, the family cannot operate successfully unless we all do our fair share. If this lesson were honestly learned it might solve many family problems!

In teaching a lesson on this subject, why not bake a family cake? Let each member of the family represent one or more ingredients and then let each one contribute the ingredient he is representing. Make sure the children understand that the cake would fail if even one thing were left out or if one ingredient were too lazy to do the job you expected of it. (Another approach—although it would ruin a good cake—is to leave out one ingredient and really show the children what would happen!)

Family Cake Recipe:

2 cups flour	This would be father—the sturdy foundation upon which the whole family is built.
1½ cups sugar	Mother would be the sugar—adding the right touch of sweetness to the home.
1 teaspoon salt	Little Tim would be the salt—what a flop our cake would be without this much-needed touch.
2 teaspoons baking powder	Big sister Sharon can be the baking powder—this family wouldn't get far without her willing and capable help.

Sift dry ingredients three
   times and add:

½ cup margarine, butter, or oil	Bob would be the butter—his sense of humor and agreeable personality add richness to our family life.
1 cup milk	Ellen is the milk—she is able to combine the abilities of the rest of the family by being where she is needed most at just the right time.
1 teaspoon vanilla	This would be baby Steven—he is still so small but gives our family a delicious flavor.

Blend and then beat in:

Two large eggs	What would we do without the eggs?!—or without our Linda. Many of our activities would fall flat, just like the cake, without her pep and enthusiasm.
Mix 2 to 3 minutes	Now the ingredients must be blended so that you can't distinguish one from the other—alone they are not much good! Only when they are combined, do they become something special.

Now bake the cake in the oven of the gospel (at 375 degrees for 25-30 minutes) to make it rise to perfection and ice it with the sweetness of love.

Goals

Sometimes people waste many years of their lives because they are not quite sure in which direction they should go. We as Latter-day Saints, should never have this problem. The Lord has revealed to us through his prophets just what the purpose of our life on earth should be. Children should understand this early in life so that they know where they are headed. They should set for themselves many goals—some small, some great, some short-range and some long-range goals—all of which should eventually lead them to the all-important goal of eternal exaltation.

It would be helpful, then, to do something with your children that will make them stop and think about what is really important and what they want out of life. One method in which this could be accomplished is through the following family activity.

Write a short biography of each family member, making an effort to include incidents they have especially enjoyed as well as their accomplishments in life so far. Then give each family member his own story to finish. (This activity is especially good for older children, but even small children would enjoy having someone else help them write theirs.) Have each one write his story just the way he hopes it will happen. Have him include school and school activities (you may discover that your small daughter has her heart set on becoming a cheer leader in high school or that your son thinks as much of being a basketball star as he does of going on a mission!), the part the Church should play in his life, a mission, when and where he would like to marry, what occupation he is interested in, etc.

Emphasize that it is his power to make this story come true! It might be a good idea to file the completed biography in a place where the child can read it occasionally so he can compare his real life with the one he hopes to have.

Following is a sample biography:

Once upon a time, not too many years ago, a very special little blond-haired, blue-eyed baby was born. Right from the first this was a happy little girl because she had parents, grandparents, relatives, and friends who loved her and took care of her. When she was still just a little baby, she learned how to crawl. Her mother remembers the very first Christmas after she was born. She was only five months old, yet she was able to get into all the Christmas presents and pull the icicles off the bottom branches of the Christmas tree. From that time on she got into all kinds of mischief, but her mother and father didn't mind too much because they knew that's how babies learn things. Do you know who this baby was? Yes, of course it was YOU!

Little by little you grew up. You got teeth, learned to walk and run and play games, learned to feed yourself, and most important of all began to learn what you could and couldn't do. When you were two, a baby sister was born, and even though you were still quite small, you helped take care of her, and you loved to play with her.

When you were old enough, you started going to Junior Sunday School and Primary, and we were so proud of you when the teachers told us what a good girl you were. You listened quietly and liked to answer the questions, and you always did what the teachers asked. You loved to go to church!

At home you were a little ray of sunshine. Sometimes you were naughty, but most of the time you tried very hard to do what was right. You have a voice like a little angel, and everyone loves to hear you sing. You are a lovely little dancer also and have started learning to play the piano. You have made everyone happy with your music.

A little baby brother was born, and by this time you were big enough to feed and tend him. Then, too, you were old enough to be a good helper at home because you had learned to do dishes, dust, vacuum, and other things. Do you remember the summers you went to nursery school, and at home how you started learning to read, do arithmetic, and tell time?

Before long you started going to school. A whole wonderful new world opened up to you here! So much to learn, so much to do, and so many new friends! You worked hard and played hard at school—so of course you have enjoyed it.

When you were eight, a very important event took place. You were baptized and confirmed a member of the Church. Bishop White talked to you about your baptism and what it meant, and also the responsibility that came with it. Your grandparents traveled many miles just to share this wonderful occasion with you, and we had a lovely dinner with the family to honor you.

Now you are even older and have many other important things to look forward to. The future years of your life hold many treasures in store for you. What would you like them to be?

Testimony Hour

One of the most impressive and valuable of any Family Home Evening activity has been our monthly testimony time. After our regular lesson from the *Church Family Home Evening Manual*, we take a little time once each month to have our children bear their testimonies. We refresh their memories first by telling them that a testimony is a feeling in your heart to help you believe the gospel is true. A testimony is also a feeling of thankfulness for blessings received from our Heavenly Father. We further help them by bearing our testimonies to them in a simple way so they have some example to guide them.

The gospel is not just a series of doctrine and scriptures. The gospel is the way of life, and it encompasses all things that are worthwhile. Family Home Evening activities can help children realize that the gospel is wonderful and workable, not dull and stuffy. The Church of Jesus Christ helps us to live a balanced life. Family fun, wholesome activities, and special projects are all part of the plan. Family Home Evening activities can do much to help children seek good times wherever they might be, love the things of life which matter most, and help build within them testimonies of the gospel.

As you prepare and conduct Family Home Evenings for your children, keep foremost in mind that people remember 90% of what they DO and plan accordingly. A person becomes the sum total of his experiences. As parents, you should not force your children to do anything or become any particular thing, but you can provide the experiences to help them do so or become so. If you want to raise a choice family, you must surround your children with choice experiences!

(For a family activity on thoughtfulness, see the Pixie Game, pages 146-147, *The Art of Teaching Children*, by Daryl V. Hoole, published by the Deseret Book Company.)

III

Flash Cards  and Flip Charts

A Chinese sage once said: "One seeing is worth ten hearings." This truth—which has been said in many ways in many languages—cannot be over-emphasized in good teaching. Certainly a vital part of our Family Home Evening lesson is appropriate, effective visual material.

Not only can visual materials help a lesson be learned, but they aid in communicating the information accurately and correctly—false impressions and misunderstandings seldom come about. Unless we are very careful, children sometimes do misunderstand things. Recently a little boy prayed: "Please bless the gospel and his two counselors."

Variety is the spice of life—and of good teaching. There are numerous types of effective visual materials, some of which will be discussed in subsequent chapters. This chapter has to do with flash cards and flip charts. Flash cards and flip charts are easy to make and easy to use. Their simplicity offers another advantage, too: even very young children can teach with them which means they are learning what the lessons are all about. Our little children love to play Sunday School or Primary with each other or with their dolls, and it's a thrill to us as parents to watch them teach with flash cards or flip charts. Older children, too, appreciate their conciseness and gain from the lasting mental image they create.

Repetition is the key to learning, understanding, and conversion. Lessons on gospel principles and values should be repeated several times a year as children grow older. It's fun and easy to review and repeat with flash cards and flip charts.

In short, flash cards and flip charts can add just the "Sugar 'n Spice" you need to teach effectively.

Flash cards are loose cards or sheets of paper which have been illustrated. Flip charts are just flash cards bound together with rings of some sort. Either can be made by you from original drawings (they needn't be professional) or from magazine picture cut-outs. Picture series depicting various phases of the gospel or ready-made flash cards or flip charts can be purchased through LDS Church book-stores.

Subjects may range from Manners to Missionary Work to Church History—anything which may help your children better understand values and principles of the gospel. Following are several sample flash card lessons to help you get started:

(For a flip chart on baptism, refer to *The Art of Teaching Children*, pages 168-175, and also the kit to the book, *The Art of Teaching Children*.)
(For a flash card lesson on reverence, refer to "A Church Creep" by Mary Ellen Jolley, available through most LDS Church bookstores.)

Priesthood

Flash card lesson to help young boys prepare themselves to hold the priesthood and to help them honor it after they have received it.

The priesthood is the authority to
act in the name of God.

" . . . no man taketh this honour unto himself, but he that is called of God, as was Aaron."
(Hebrews 5:4.)

The priesthood was restored to the earth.

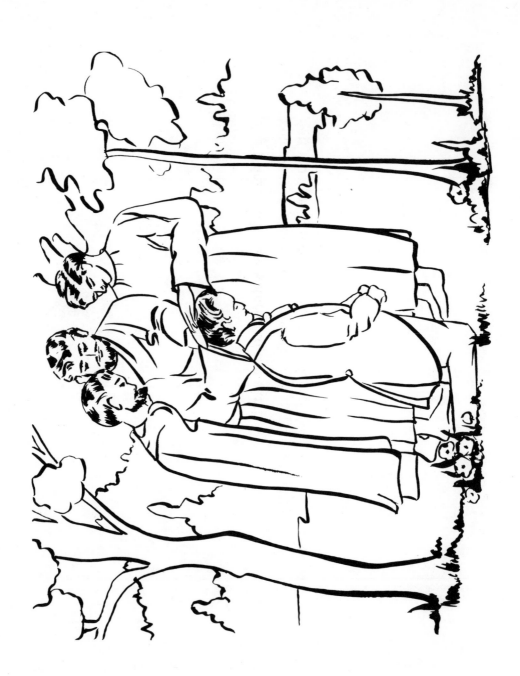

Worthy male members of the Church may receive the priesthood.
YOU (to a boy) may receive the priesthood.

You must be at least twelve years of age.
You must be a member of the Church in good standing.
You must be interviewed by the bishop.

You must be sustained by the ward membership.

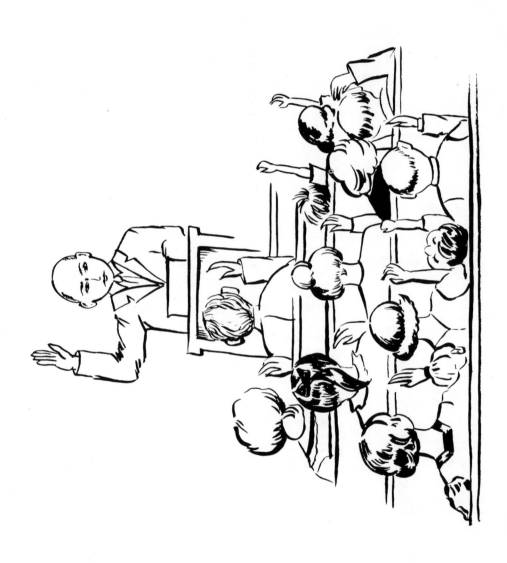

You then report to a priesthood quorum where you are ordained to the Aaronic Priesthood and the office of deacon. Later you may be given the office of teacher and then of priest.

The duties of a deacon are to pass the Sacrament, collect fast offerings, and assist the bishop in whatever way he can.

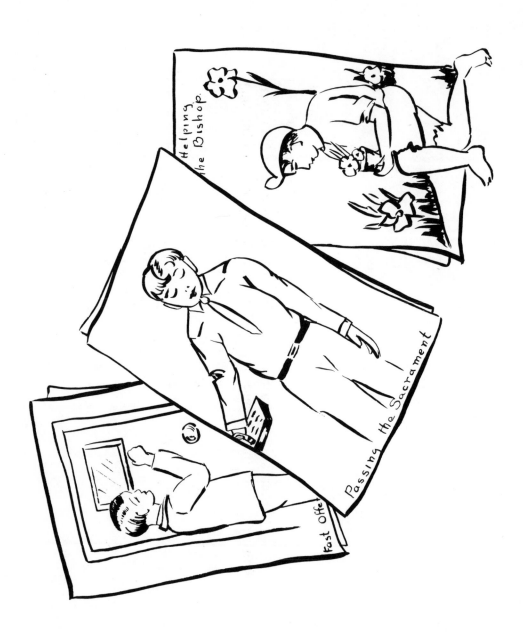

The teachers are the Watchmen of the Church. They are to visit the homes of the members once a month, inquire into the needs of the people, and teach them the will of God. They are to be ushers or doorkeepers, care for meetinghouses, act as messengers for the bishop, and assist the deacons.

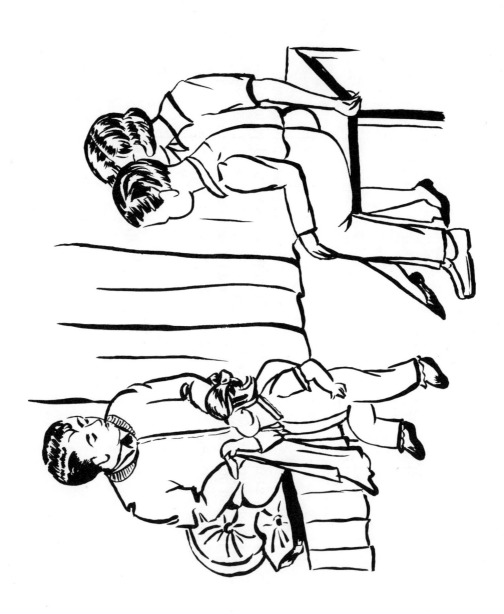

Priests have the authority to administer to the Sacrament, baptize, and ordain other priests, teachers, and deacons.

Your general responsibilities as a bearer of the priesthood are:

to live the commandments of Heavenly Father.

to attend church meetings and be on time and be prepared

to fulfil your assignment.

to remain in the meeting until its conclusion—not just wait until the ordinance is completed then duck out.

to be reverent.

to have an attitude compatible with the power of God which is yours.

Your blessings as a bearer of the priesthood are numerous. Some of them would include:

power to bless and serve others through the priesthood.

growth and development in the kingdom of God.

worthiness to receive Higher or Melchizedek Priesthood, when you become of age.

preparation for a temple marriage.

privilege of being patriarch in your own family some day.

following the road which leads to eternal family life and joy and blessings forever.

THE DISTINCTIVE FEATURES OF THE CHURCH
OF JESUS CHRIST OF LATTER-DAY SAINTS

Each time our family drives along South Temple Street in Salt Lake City with its impressive looking churches and cathedrals, children invariably ask questions such as these: "What does that church teach?" "Is that a true church?" "Why is our church the only true church?" "Why is our church different?" "What makes our church so special?" Or, as our four-year-old puts it: "Is that a smoking church?"

In attempting to answer these questions, my thoughts have gone back to the time I served as secretary to Elder Adam S. Bennion of the Council of the Twelve. I remember well the choice experience which was mine as I observed him develop one of his great speeches: "What Is Distinctive about Mormonism?" I watched that talk grow from six or eight distinctive features to the twenty-three features Elder Bennion presented in general conference, April 1957. (For additional information on Elder Bennion's talk, "What Is Distinctive about Mormonism?" refer to *The Improvement Era*, June 1957, page 433, or to the pamphlet by the same name published by the Deseret Book Company.)

We have found that a flash card lesson built around some of the distinctive features of the Church has helped our children understand and appreciate the place The Church of Jesus Christ of Latter-day Saints holds in the world. Such a lesson has been a testimony-building one in our family. It can be in your family, too.

It would be well to help children understand that since the restoration of the gospel in 1830, every major change in the Christian churches of the world has been towards our LDS beliefs. Some churches are endeavoring to promote among their membership such principles as tithing, correct concept of Deity, lay leadership, and laws of health. This is another evidence of the fact that we are doing things in the right way, in the way of our Father in heaven. The time may come when the only distinguishing feature of The Church of Jesus Christ will be the authority. The authority is the great and important distinguishing feature.

The explanation which accompanies each distinctive feature can range from a simple statement for the very youngest children to a detailed discussion for older children. The list of distinctive features can be varied in length, depending on the age of the children who are being taught. Wise parents will add to this list over the years and will repeat the lesson many times so that their children can know for themselves why our Church is so special—why it is the restored Church of Jesus Christ.

Following are a few of the basic distinctive features of the Church to help this lesson. (Other features, such as the welfare plan, our great pioneer story, our program for the youth, the Home Teaching program may be added as you see fit.)

Explanation

1. A Wonderful Concept of Deity

We know who God is and understand our relationship to him. "And this is life eternal, that they might know thee the only true God and Jesus Christ, whom thou hast sent."

(John 17:3.)

2. *The Priesthood.*

The priesthood is the authority to act in the name of God. Because of the restoration of the gospel, the keys of the priesthood have been returned to the earth, and the righteous boys and men of the Church may hold the priesthood.

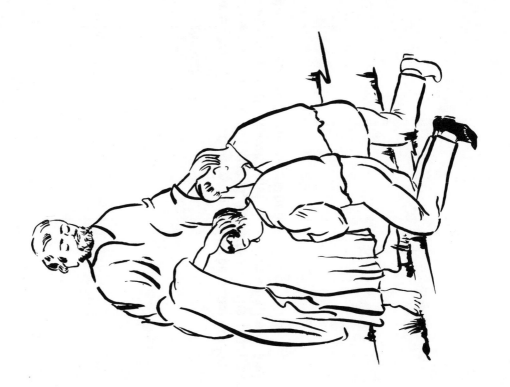

3. *A Wonderful Organization*

"We believe in the same organization that existed in the Primitive Church, viz., apostles, prophets, pastors, teachers, evangelists etc."

(Sixth Article of Faith.)

We also believe that every member of the Church—not just a few especially trained individuals—may serve and work in the Church so that each person may benefit from the growth, development, and blessings of service.

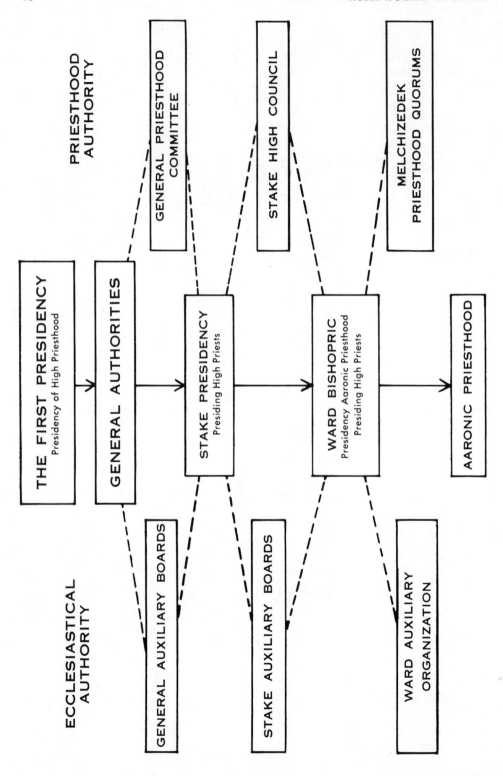

4. *Continuing Revelation*

"We believe all that God has revealed, all that He does now reveal, and we believe that He will yet reveal many great and important things pertaining to the kingdom of God."

(Ninth Article of Faith.)

The Book of Mormon is the Second Witness for Christ and gives us information so we may better understand the Bible. The Book of Mormon also tells us of the origin of the American Indians.

The Pearl of Great Price discloses marvelous truths concerning the plan of our Father in heaven and helps us more fully understand the gospel. (The origin of the Pearl of Great Price isn't too well known among the young children of the Church and would make a fascinating story at this point.)

The Doctrine and Covenants tells us the will of the Lord concerning our latter-day times and gives information for the building up of the kingdom of God in this dispensation.

5. *Temples and Temple Ordinances*

Through temple work we have answers to the three great questions: (1) Where did we come from? (2) Why are we here? (3) Where are we going? When we go through the temple, we may be married for time and eternity and receive endowments which prepare us for eternal life. Also, through temple ordinances we are able to do work for the dead, so that people who have passed on without hearing of the gospel may have a chance to accept baptism and endowment work.

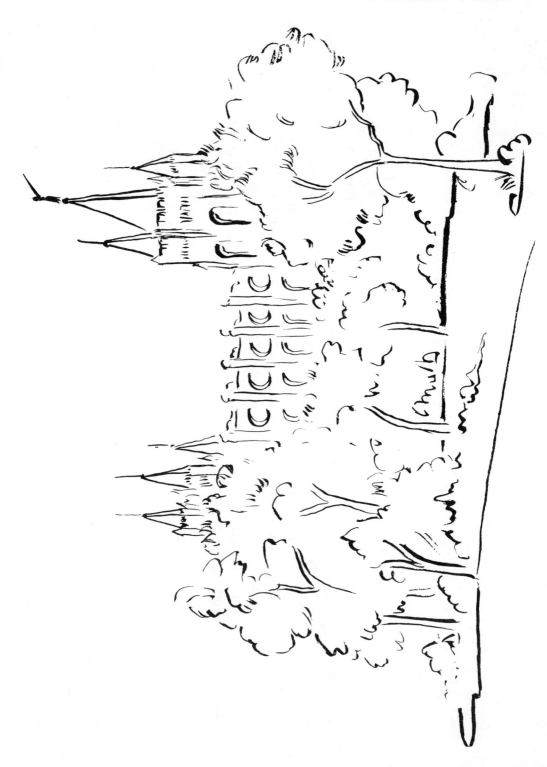

6. *Tithing*

Tithing is the Lord's way of financing his kingdom on earth. We are to return one tenth of our increase to the Lord.

7. The Word of Wisdom

Through revelation we have been given a divine health law to help us enjoy physical health and spiritual growth.

8. *The Missionary System*

Many thousands of LDS men and women go out into the world at their own expense for two to two-and-a-half years to share their testimony and teach the gospel.

THE PRESIDENTS OF THE CHURCH

THE PRESIDENTS OF THE CHURCH

1. The greatest difference between The Church of Jesus Christ of Latter-day Saints and all other churches in existence today is the fact that our Church is led by a living prophet of God who receives continuous inspiration to the Lord's work here on earth.

2. This prophet holds the keys to the priesthood which gives him authority to act in the name of God. As you can see, the man who guides our Church must be a very remarkable and righteous person. The Lord himself chooses his prophets, so we can be sure that a mistake is never made. History has shown us that the man leading the Church has always been the most qualified to handle the responsibilities and meet the needs of the time. Each of our prophets has had a great mission to perform, and even though they have all been different, each has contributed something of lasting value to the Church.

JOSEPH SMITH

First President

He established the fulness of the everlasting gospel and organized the Church of Jesus Christ upon the earth.

Photos of the Presidents of the
Church courtesy of The Improvement Era.

BRIGHAM YOUNG

Second President

He was known as a great organizer, leader, and colonizer. He led the Saints to the West and established Salt Lake City and many other communities.

JOHN TAYLOR

Third President

He was called the "Champion of Liberty." His ability as a writer and publisher was of great value to the Church. As its President, he stimulated the missionary work by calling more missionaries out than ever before.

WILFORD WOODRUFF

Fourth President

He was called "Wilford the Faithful." His life was spared many times as a child and he was one of the church's greatest missionaries. While President, the Salt Lake Temple was dedicated, and Utah became a state.

LORENZO SNOW

Fifth President

He was among the first to establish cooperative enterprises in Utah. As President of the Church, he brought about great financial improvements in the Church through emphasizing the law of tithing.

JOSEPH F. SMITH

Sixth President

He became a missionary at 15 and served as a Counselor to three Presidents. As President, he instituted a large building program including the Alberta and Hawaiian temples. He had an interest in early landmarks of the Church and purchased some of these. Under his guidance the Church became debt-free, and he also encouraged the individual members to keep out of debt.

HEBER J. GRANT

Seventh President

During the administration of Heber J. Grant, much opposition and prejudice against the Church was broken down. He was acquainted with many influential people of the nation and was in this way a great missionary for the Church. It was under his leadership that the great welfare program was inaugurated.

GEORGE ALBERT SMITH

Eighth President

President Smith was known as "The Disciple of Love." He traveled many thousands of miles in behalf of the Church. He was also a great Scouter, and received the Silver Buffalo award— the highest award in scouting.

DAVID O. McKAY

Ninth President

Under the leadership of President McKay, all programs of the Church have expanded. He has been a great missionary and traveler, and five temples have been built and dedicated while he has been President. His great messages to the Church have emphasized love and happiness in the home and teaching children the gospel.

DILLY THE DAWDLER

Dilly was a fine little person—except for one terrible habit. Dilly was a Dawdler. His only speed was too s-l-o-w. Dilly was late for breakfast every morning because instead of jumping out of bed when he had had enough sleep, he would lie in bed and daydream and daydream and daydream.

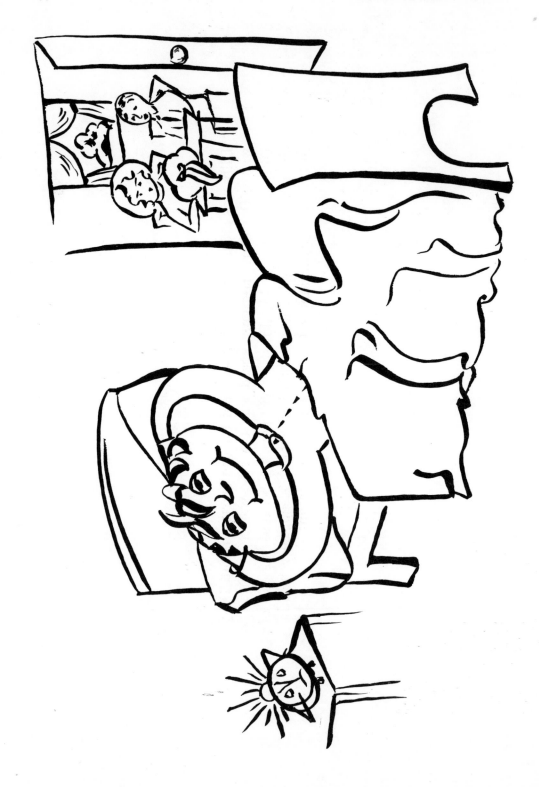

Washing and dressing, which should take only a few minutes, sometimes took Dilly an hour because he would walk from room to room, stop to play with the cat, look out the window, and do almost anything but put his clothes on.

Dilly's friends usually had to wait for him, and sometimes they would leave for school without him. A few times Dilly was even tardy for school.

Dilly was a Dawdler at school, too, and often while the other children would be out playing at recess, Dilly would be in the classroom still trying to finish his work.

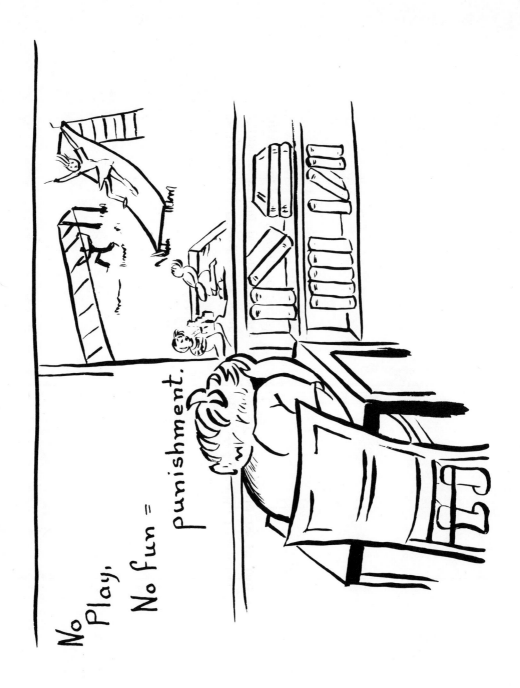

No Play,
No Fun =
Punishment.

Dilly missed lots of fun each summer because it would take him all morning to get his chores done. The other children in the neighborhood had done their work and had been riding their bikes, skating, or playing games for several hours.

It was an unhappy life for Dilly. He was tired of being scolded and hurried and reminded. He was tired of being too late for the fun and good times. He wondered what to do.

Dilly's mother told him that his dawdling was just a bad habit. Habits are formed when we do the same thing over and over again. Each time we do something, it's like wrapping another piece of thread around us until we are all bound up. Dilly had been a dawdler for so long that he was tied up tight with being too slow. Dilly felt there were so many threads around him that he just couldn't break them.

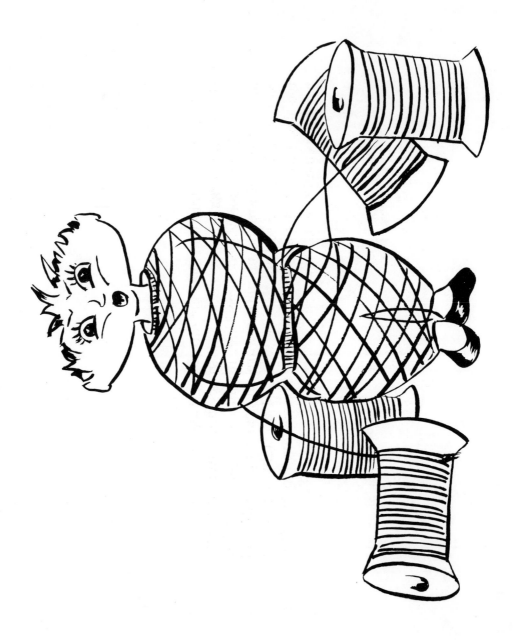

Dilly's mother suggested that the best way to break a bad habit is to begin unwinding the threads, one by one. Dilly decided the first thread which should be unwound was the one for lying in bed too long in the mornings. He made up his mind to get out of bed on time for three mornings in a row. The fourth morning he found himself out of bed on time without even thinking about it. That thread had been unwound! Then Dilly decided for the next three mornings he would work quickly until he was completely washed and dressed. He surprised himself by learning how much easier it was to get dressed quickly than it was to take too long. Soon he found that thread was completely unwound, too!

By the end of another week, Dilly had unwound so many of his bad habit threads that he could break the few which were left with one try. Dilly was free! He was no longer tied up with the bad habit of being a dawdler.

Which one are you—Dilly the Dawdler or Dilly who is free?

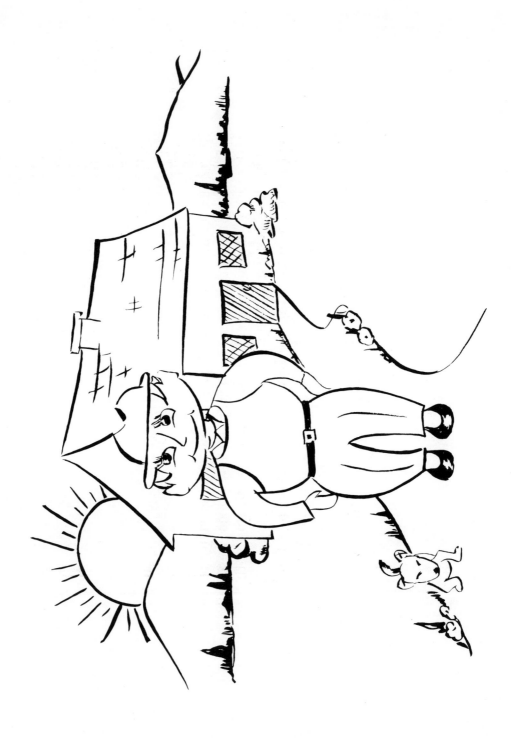

IV

Flannel  Board Lessons

The flannel board is one of the most popular, versatile, and effective types of visual materials. It offers a creative challenge in teaching, and parents can use it to help a lesson be very impressive in the minds of children of all ages. As some "Sugar 'n Spice" to help put over a lesson, it's great! Following are two sample flannel board lessons. (To prepare these lessons for your flannel board cut out the figures and adhere a strip of flannel, sandpaper, or suede paper to the backs of them. When the figures aren't in use, keep them in the envelope pasted in the back of this book.)

HARRY THE HERRING

(Scene I)

Excitement is everywhere in the little Dutch fishing village. The women are wearing their Sunday best. Their lace caps are covering thin sheets of gold that would glitter brightly if only the sun would come out. Fresh, clean aprons are donned for the occasion and black shawls have been exchanged for brighter colors. Today no group of fishermen is standing about talking and swapping "fish stories." Children are running here and there, some trying to help, nearly all are in the way. Their wooden shoes clatter on the bricks and cobblestones. Both harbors are filled with fishing boats and, from a distance, it seems to be a complicated network of ropes, masts, and flags. Banners of every color, kind, size, and shape are flying gaily, and the

red, white, and blue of the Dutch flag can be seen everywhere. In the streets, throngs of spectators have gathered to watch the boats sail for the first time of the year. Ice cream and herring vendors add to the turmoil and the fun. Hundreds and hundreds of barrels line the shore. The fishermen are busy loading them onto the boats, and the nets are rolled up and ready to go. And so, amid the music of bands and street organs, the first boat sails. Along with good-byes and wishes of good luck from the women and children, the other boats follow with their banners waving to and fro in the wind. As the boats leave the shelter of the harbor, they bounce about on the waves and look as if they might topple over. One by one they parade along the coast and finally become just specks on the horizon. The boats are headed out to sea where they will cast their nets— miles and miles of nets into the waters to catch thousands and thousands of fish. And the first boat back home will have the honor of presenting a barrel of herring to the Queen! And so the fishing season begins happily in the village.

(Scene II)

But down underneath the waves of the sea, something quite different is taking place. Grandfather Herring, swimming slowly among the sea shells and coral with the help of his sea-weed cane, has called a meeting of all the little herring. He, too, knows that spring has come and that the fishing boats are on their way. And he knows that the little herring must be warned!

(Scene III)

All the little herring were grumbling just a little bit as they assembled for the meeting. They had been having such a wonderful time playing hide-and-go-seek. The sea is full of wondrous places to hide and it is their very favorite game. Couldn't Grandfather Herring have waited and had the meeting another time? Of course, the little herring wouldn't have complained if they had known how important it was to be warned about the fishing boats!

As Grandfather approached, the herring stopped their chattering and made sure their tails stopped swishing and their

fins didn't rustle, for he demanded absolute quiet when he spoke. Grandfather Herring smoothed his beard and began:

"My dear little herring," he said gravely. "Up until now, you have known nothing but fun in your short lives. You have spent your days playing games and exploring. But now that spring has come, I must tell you about your greatest and most dangerous enemy." Then Grandfather told the little herring about the approaching fishing boats and about the many nets they would drop into the ocean to catch fish with.

The little herring were so frightened and amazed that they forgot all about being quiet. They started whispering and even talking out loud to each other. "What shall we do"— "What can we do"—"Oh, dear, what will happen to us" they were saying.

Grandfather Herring blew bubbles to get their attention again. "I'll tell you what you can do, for this is why I have called you together. I have lived through many fishing seasons, and I know just how to keep from being caught." When the little herring heard this, they stopped their talking to listen.

"If you will just remember one rule, you will never be caught in the nets. The rule is: NEVER LOSE YOUR TEM-PER. For as soon as you lose your temper, your cheeks will swell up, and you will not be able to get out of the net. So you see, even if you are caught in the fishermen's nets, if you just remember not to get angry but take time to think about things carefully, you will be able to wiggle free of the net. But as soon as you forget and get angry, you will not be able to get out. Losing one's temper is fatal to herring, and, I might add, also to people, for whenever someone loses his temper, he does and says things he doesn't mean, and even if he is sorry afterwards, he can't undo the damage he has done. Besides, we all look and act so foolish when we are angry, and it never solves any problems—in fact, it always makes more problems."

(Scene IV)

Grandfather dismissed the meeting and left the little herring by themselves to talk about what they had heard. "That doesn't sound so hard," said little Harvey Herring to his cousin

Harry Herring. "If that's all that we need to remember, I'm sure I'll never get caught."

"I'm not so sure," Harry replied, as they slowly swam away. "If it were really that easy, the fishermen wouldn't catch as many herring as they do every year. I think I'd better start practising right now to avoid getting angry at things. I often get angry at my brothers and sisters if they do things I don't like, and I sometimes get angry at my friends if they don't play the games that I want to play. I think it is just a bad habit with me. I'm afraid I might forget and get angry at just the wrong time."

"Well, you do what you want," said Harvey as he darted off to play with the others. "I'm not going to worry about it."

Grandfather Herring hadn't called the meeting a day too soon. For that very night, the fishing boats came and filled the sea with nets. And even though the herring had all been warned, many of them forgot the warning just long enough to get caught. As soon as they felt the net around their necks, it would make them so angry that their cheeks would swell up, and then they couldn't possibly squirm out of the net. Many of Harvey's and Harry's playmates and cousins were caught.

(Scene V)

One day Harvey and Harry were searching for a very special kind of sea shell together. They were so busy looking at shells that they didn't even see the big octopus nearby until they ran right into him. My goodness! They were frightened. Both Harvey and Harry turned around as fast as they could and swam away. They were so worried about the octopus that they didn't watch where they were going and suddenly they both felt the dreaded fish net around them! Harvey forgot all about what his grandfather had told him, and sure enough, he got angry. Up puffed his cheeks and no matter how hard he wiggled and squirmed, he couldn't get out of the net. But Harry, who had really been trying not to get angry ever—not even at his brothers and sisters—remembered just in time what Grandfather had said. He stayed very calm and thought carefully, and then, quick as a wink, he was able to squirm free and swim away.

Harry felt very bad about Harvey getting caught as well as so many of the others. But they had all been told that getting angry only makes things worse.

(Scene VI)

Harry was very glad that he had remembered and because he was so careful never to lose his temper, he lived happily through many fishing seasons. And one spring Harry became the Grandfather Herring of the sea, and it was he who called the meeting when the fishing season came to warn all the little herring!

Which just goes to show that a successful herring—or person—never loses his temper and gets all puffed up in a rage!

LITTLE DEER

(Scene I)

Swift Eagle proudly watched the roly-poly little papoose play on the wigwam floor with a brightly colored ball. No matter where the ball rolled, the little one was able to find it. But he always stayed far away from the fire where his mother, Morning Sun, was fixing supper.

Swift Eagle loved his son. They called him Little Deer now, but he would receive another name later on when he was older. For it was an Indian custom to give a baby a temporary name when he was born, and then choose a permanent name for him later on—a name that would describe his personality or his accomplishments. "I wonder," thought Swift Eagle to himself, "what kind of name my son will earn. Perhaps the name will emphasize great intelligence or honesty or trust. Or maybe, like my name, it will be given to him for his athletic ability or physical development. It is even possible he may receive a name to describe his personality like his mother's name describes hers. I wonder . . . I wonder. . . ." And Swift Eagle continued contentedly to watch Little Deer play until dinner was ready.

(Scene II)

Several years passed, and Little Deer was now able to help his mother and learn the many things that children must. He and his little cousins gathered sticks for the fire, and they were taught to be silent and respectful before older people. Little Deer also loved playing games, and he spent many happy hours having fun. "He is so full of laughter always," thought Swift Eagle one day, "maybe we should name him Laughing Waters."

(Scene III)

But as more years passed, Little Deer changed. He was still full of laughter but was also very serious about his tasks. When he was eight, he was allowed to follow his father at his work. In this way he began learning about the man's work he would one day have to do. In the evenings, he would sit with the men around the fire. He loved to hear them talk of their hunting adventures. He could hardly wait until he was old enough to go with them. During these evenings, his father taught him much about carving and told him many things he would have to know to be a successful hunter. Little Deer listened intently to everything his father said, and when he could find time, spent many hours practising. Swift Eagle noted proudly that Little Deer worked harder and better than any of the other young Indian boys. "He will become a skilled hunter and a great leader among the people," Swift Eagle thought with satisfaction. "He will earn the respect and admiration of all the others because of his industry. Perhaps he will be named for this."

(Scene IV)

Little Deer continued to develop into a fine young brave, and he was soon allowed to accompany the men on some of their shorter hunting trips. Swift Eagle was not the only one to notice how well Little Deer did on these occasions—many of the other men noticed it also and talked about it. The time was approaching when Little Deer and the other braves his age were to receive their permanent names. Their fathers spent much time discussing this among themselves as they tried to decide upon a worthy name for their sons. "I'm afraid Gray Cloud would be an appropriate name for my son," said Running Wolf sadly one night. "He is always so sullen and unhappy." "I, too, am disappointed," said Lone Bear. "It seems that Lazy One would be the most fitting name for my son."

Swift Eagle was grateful for Little Deer. There were many good names he would be worthy of, for he had tried all his life to do his best in everything. Choosing a name for Little Deer would only be difficult because of his many good qualities. It was hard to know which was the most outstanding.

(Scene V)

One evening as the men returned to the village, something happened that could have been a terrible tragedy. The women were busy preparing supper, and the older children ran to meet the hunting party. With so much going on, no one was left to watch the small children as they played. Suddenly a child crawled too close to a fire, and within seconds his clothing was aflame. As everyone else hesitated for just a moment, Little Deer ran to the child's rescue. Without pausing for even a second, he stamped out the flames and kept the child from being seriously harmed. The entire village was grateful for Little Deer's swift action and for his courage. Yet no one was surprised, for they had seen Little Deer's character develop for many years, and they knew that he would always be equal to any challenge he met.

When it was finally time for Little Deer to receive his permanent name, there were many good things about him to be considered. He had a cheerful disposition, he was industrious, he became a skilful hunter, he was respected by the entire village, and he displayed great courage and character.

Think for a moment—if you were to select a name for Little Deer, what would you choose? (Have family suggest names they think would be good).

What would happen if we followed this Indian custom? What kind of name would you deserve—what name would best describe your character? Would you have to be satisfied with a name such as Gray Cloud or Lazy One? Or are you best known for good things, as Little Deer was?

(For a flannelboard lesson on the Plan of Salvation, see *The Art of Teaching Children*, pages 198-210, and also the kit to *The Art of Teaching Children*.)

V
Puppets

All too often in teaching we try to hold a child's attention before we get it. We would like to recommend a great attention-getter to you. It's PUPPETS! Little toddlers are fascinated by the puppets' movements, growing children find anything they say impressive and memorable, and even teenagers and adults are charmed by them. Anything a puppet says is far more eloquent than the well-worn teachings so often heard from parents. Their third party influence just can't be over-estimated! Because of this, puppets rank among the great teachers of all time and frequently add just the touch of "Sugar 'n Spice" needed to make a lesson impressive.

Puppets can be easily made in a number of different ways. Paper bags or socks (with faces painted on them) placed over one's hand are the simplest of all. Potato or papier-mache heads or styrofoam balls for heads make them a little more special. Inexpensive doll faces can be purchased from hobby stores. When these faces are stitched to fabric heads, hats, and bag-like bodies, they make cute puppets. For a more professional puppet, patterns can be secured for a completely fabric puppet. Clever puppets can also be purchased commercially.

It takes little skill to work with puppets—some of our best puppet lessons have been given by our young children with their own original stories and lesson ideas. (If a child's fingers are too short to manipulate the puppet, have him insert a spoon handle in the puppet's head.) All one must remember is that the puppet who is speaking waves his arms or nods his head as he does so. The other puppet or puppets on the scene are to be motionless until their turn to speak. A cardboard box decorated by the children makes a fine puppet stage. Also, puppet demonstrations can be effective with the puppets appearing from behind a couch or arm chair.

Almost any story can be adapted for puppets by just developing a simple dialogue. It can be very challenging and satisfying to parents to create some original puppet stories to meet needs in teaching their children. Children love to give puppet lessons to each other and to their dolls, and the sermons they preach are remarkable! Following are sample lessons which have helped our children. We feel it can be of value in your family, too, because after all, if a puppet says so, it's great!

The Winning Way

SCENE I:

BRUCE: Hi, Gary, where are you going in such a hurry?

GARY: Oh, hello, Bruce. Mr. Stevens from the grocery store just called. He needs some extra help today and asked if I would like the job.

BRUCE: Is that all that's making you feel so enthusiastic? Golly, who wants to spend his Saturday working in a grocery store . . . I'm glad nobody ever calls me for a job.

GARY: Well, I like it. I have to earn only five more dollars and I'll have enough money for swimming lessons this summer. Besides, the last time I worked for Mr. Stevens he said I had done so well that he gave me an extra 50c for the day. I can't pass up a chance like this. By the way, what are you going to do today?

BRUCE: Who, me? Oh, I don't know. I'll just ride around on my bike until I find something to do.

GARY: Well, okay. I'll see you later. Oh, wait a minute. Next week we're to register for swimming lessons. Why don't you take lessons with me? You're ready for the advanced class by now, aren't you?

BRUCE: I guess so, but I can't see much reason to go on with lessons. I can paddle around a little bit. Besides, when it's hot I just don't feel like doing anything. Have fun at the grocery store, ha ha! See you later.

Scene II: Next Week

GARY: What's the matter, Bruce? You look terrible.

BRUCE: Aw, I'm all right. It's just that these report card days always put me down in the dumps.

GARY: Bad marks, is that right?

BRUCE: Yeah, and besides that I got several unsatisfactory checks in my citizenship. I wonder who that old Miss Ryan thinks she is. She claims that I don't use my time well and that my work isn't as good as I could do. Gee, what do people expect of one guy? Does she pick on you, too, Gary?

GARY: Now, Bruce, you don't really think Miss Ryan would pick on anyone. I bet we get just what we deserve.

BRUCE: Yeah, you can say that because you probably got top marks in everything.

GARY: That's right, Bruce, I did get good marks, but I worked hard for them.

BRUCE: I'll have to admit, you do work hard, but it seems easy for you to do so.

GARY: I guess that's because I'm used to it. My mom has had me working ever since I can remember. Every morning she gives me a list of chores to do, and she makes me stick with them until they're done right. She really expects a a lot of me and makes certain that I work to the best of my ability.

BRUCE: Ugh, what a life. I never do anything at home but watch TV. My mother keeps saying I should keep up my room, but all she does is talk about it so I don't get very worried. Oh, last week I did try to wash the car, but Dad said it looked worse after I was through than it did before.

GARY: Boy, if that had been at my home, my dad would have worked with me until I knew how to make it sparkle.

BRUCE: What are your parents trying to do to you, anyway? Don't you ever have any freedom or time for fun?

GARY: Oh, sure. I gripe about all the work sometimes, but really it's surprising how many hours are left after my chores and studying are done. I have lots of time for cub scouting. I just finished my 19th model airplane. I've got a collection of them in my room. I'm going camping Friday night with my older brothers. Mmmm, I can taste those juicy hot dogs already. Oh, and right now I've been repainting the tree house I built last year. You should see how neat it's going to be. Really, I have lots of fun. Dad tells me that my duties around the home and yard really help me to have more extra time because they teach me to use my time better. My folks were explaining all this to some friends the other night. I didn't understand everything, but the people seemed very pleased when Dad told them about the cow we just bought. He said, "Gary milks the cow in the morning to save him, and I milk the cow at night to save the cow!"

BRUCE: Your parents are really strict. Mine don't seem to care what I do. I don't think I care, either. All they do is punish me when I'm too noisy and take my temperature when I'm too quiet.

GARY: It's my dinner time. Sorry about your report card. See you later.

SCENE III: Summer Vacation

BRUCE: Hi, Gary, what are you doing now?

GARY: Hi, come on and help. Dad said when these weeds are pulled he'd take me swimming. How about pulling a few weeds yourself. I bet Dad would take you swimming, too.

BRUCE: Well . . . okay, it's a deal.

GARY: (still pulling weeds) Where are you going on your vacation this year, Bruce?

BRUCE: Oh, we aren't going anywhere. My folks say we can't afford it.

GARY: That's too bad. We're going to Disneyland and the beach in California. I guess we couldn't afford it, either, except that all of us children have been saving some of our money since last year and are contributing toward the trip. Mother says when we all work together, wonderful things can happen. We've had some great trips this way before. I can hardly wait to go this year.

BRUCE: Wow, that really sounds fun. How do you earn your money?

GARY: My two older brothers have part-time jobs, and my sister goes baby sitting and helps a lady with her ironing. I've got a paper route, and as you'll remember I help out at the grocery store once in a while. During the summertime I mow lawns and do yard work around the neighborhood. My little sister puts up the lunches for all of us and earns some money that way.

BRUCE: Do you have to donate all your money to family projects or do you have any to spend, too?

GARY: Oh, I have some to spend. Dad has helped me work out a budget. I always put ten percent of my money away for tithing. Then I put some into my mission fund bank. Part of it goes for family trips and birthday and Christmas presents. I spend the rest on new models, treats from the store, special things I need, and stuff like that. Here goes the last weed. Let's go tell my dad we're ready for a swim.

SCENE IV: Fall Day after School

BRUCE: Gary! That's real swell that you've been elected president of our class. You'll be great.

GARY: Thanks, I'll sure do my best. How are things with you?

BRUCE: You know, Gary, I've been thinking a lot about you lately. To be honest, I used to think you were the most picked-on, overworked fellow I knew. But I can see now that you get out of life just what you put into it. You have great times with your family. Everybody likes you, and you have lots of friends. You know how to work well and earn money. You get the best grades, and you always have fun, interesting things to do. Now, I'm the guy I feel sorry for. Nothing special ever happens to me. I'm sure it's because I never put forth any special effort. I'd give a lot to be like you, Gary. How can I do it?

GARY: That's a real big question, Bruce. Maybe one way would be to have my folks talk to your parents and tell them some of the things we do in our family. They could tell your mother and father how you feel.

BRUCE: Gee, that's a great idea!

"Remember the Sabbath Day . . ."

This type of puppet show is a little different because only one puppet is used. The dialogue takes place, unrehearsed, between one puppet and a child or children. Because you don't know in advance what the child will say, it is impossible to prepare a script in advance. Even though the entire dialogue can't be written, you should write down the important points you want to cover to make sure everything is brought in that should be. The puppet can often lead the child.

You should keep in mind that the purpose of a one-puppet show is not to teach new information but to give a child an opportunity to reinforce his ideas on a subject he is familiar with. It also teaches him how to explain to others why he believes as he does. In addition it gives you the chance to see how your child really does feel and how well he understands a subject.

Here is a sample of what might take place: (You can either tell the child in advance what is going to happen, or you can simply tell him he is to pretend that it is Sunday morning and that he is on his way to Sunday School. As he starts on his way, let the puppet pop out from behind a chair and surprise him.)

WILLIAM: Hi there! My name is William. We just moved into the new house down the street. Can I be your friend?

CHILD: Sure you can.

WILLIAM: What's your name?

CHILD: Steven. And this is my house right here.

WILLIAM: You must be going somewhere special—you're all dressed up. Is there a party or something?

CHILD: I'm going to Sunday School. Do you want to come with me?

WILLIAM: Gee whiz, no. I almost never go to church. What do you do there?

CHILD: We sing and pray, take the Sacrament, have lessons and stories, and sometimes we make things.

WILLIAM: Do you like Sundays?

CHILD: Oh, yes. Sunday is one of my favorite days.

WILLIAM: It is? How come?

CHILD: Because I like to go to Sunday School and Sacrament meeting, and our family always does special things together on Sunday.

WILLIAM: I remember that somebody told me that Sunday is the Lord's day. What does that mean?

CHILD: That means that Sunday is the day we worship the Lord and rest from our work.

WILLIAM: Well, I guess that isn't so bad—especially the resting part. Dad told me this morning I have to mow the lawn before I can do anything else. I guess if I hurry, I'll be through with that by the time you get home from Sunday School. Then maybe we could go swimming together or to a show. Would you like to do that?

CHILD: Tomorrow, maybe, but not today, thank you. I never do anything like that on Sundays.

WILLIAM: Why not? That's not work!

CHILD: I know it, but remember, Sunday is the Lord's day. We have six other days to do our work and have fun.

WILLIAM: Well, what do you do all day, then?

CHILD: After Sunday School and dinner, our family usually does something together. Sometimes we read stories or mother helps us with quiet activities. Today we are going to visit my grandmother, and we'll probably get home just in time to go to Sacrament meeting.

WILLIAM: You mean, you have to go to another meeting, too? What do you do there?

CHILD: Special speakers talk to us about the gospel and try to help us to live better. Sometimes, like tonight, a missionary talks. That's my favorite because I want to be a missionary someday.

WILLIAM: I don't know if I'd like to go to two meetings. Still I guess Sunday should be special. It's just like any other day to me. My parents usually take me to church at Easter and Christmas and sometimes other days, but I don't go often enough to understand very much about it. But I have been wondering about my Heavenly Father lately. Do you think it's important to know about religion?

CHILD: Oh, yes. If we didn't understand the gospel, we wouldn't know how we are supposed to live.

WILLIAM: I wonder if my parents would let me go with you next Sunday. Would your Sunday School teacher care if I came?

CHILD: Of course not. She always tells us to bring our friends.

WILLIAM: I wonder when I'd get the lawn mowed, though, if I went to church on Sundays. When do you do your chores?

CHILD: I have to finish my chores on Saturday before I can play. One of the most important things we do at our house on Saturday is get ready for Sunday. We all get our work done on that day so we can keep the Sabbath day holy.

WILLIAM: I wish our family would do that. I think I'd like Sundays better if they were special. But you had better hurry and go now, or else you'll be late.

CHILD: All right, but if you'll come over tomorrow, we'll play together. And be sure and plan on going to church with me next week.

(For a puppet show presentation on honesty, see *The Art of Teaching Children*, pages 134-141.)

VI
Games

Games are fun! Games are good family activities! Games are wholesome entertainment! Games are educational! A game may be just the bit of "Sugar 'n Spice" needed to add liveliness to a lesson. Children, young and old, will sit up and take notice when you say, "Let's play a game."

Most games are not enough in themselves to be an entire lesson, but they serve many other purposes. A game may be used to get attention, or to set a mood, or to prepare a way to teach. A game adds variety to lessons. A game serves as a good review of previous lessons. A game may be an excellent summary of a current lesson or it may be used right in the middle of a lesson to spark enthusiasm. The value of games should not be overlooked.

Keep in mind, however, that these games are not just to be entertaining. They should also be learning experiences. And the important thing is not only to play the game well—the real emphasis should be on how the knowledge or ideas obtained can be applied in one's life.

Experienced teachers say that to teach successfully they must first get their students off balance. Children naturally resist teaching sometimes, so they will be much more approachable if they are caught off guard a little. A game is the ideal solution to this problem.

In this chapter are some games you may wish to adapt to the needs of your family or perhaps they will give you ideas to develop new games.

Quizzes

Quizzes are always popular. Following is a quiz on values that can lead to a lively discussion and stimulate thinking as well as prepare children to face these similar real-life situations as they should. Children like a chance to express their opinions and this would give them such an opportunity.

Values Quiz

1. Susan was getting ready to go to Sunday School when her next-door neighbor called her on the telephone. The neighbor quickly explained that their baby was seriously ill and must be taken 50 miles to the nearest hospital immediately. Would Susan please come and care for the other children for several hours? Susan knew this would ruin her perfect attendance record at Sunday School—something she had worked hard for. If you were Susan, what would you do?

2. While taking a test at school, your teacher is unexpectedly called out of the room for a few minutes. Your best friend turns around to ask you for an answer to one of the test questions. You know he will be mad if you refuse to give him the answer—especially since many others in the room are exchanging answers while the teacher is gone. Which is most important—honesty or friendship?

3. At school some money was stolen from a locker. The principal has called your entire class into his office and asked for information regarding this incident. You know who took the money. What would you do?

4. You have received an invitation to a birthday party and would love to go. However, the party is being held the same time as your Primary. What would you do?

5. You have promised Mrs. Green to baby sit Saturday night. You have been saving your baby tending money for a very worthwhile cause, and you need several more dollars. Mrs. Taylor calls and also asks you to baby tend. You know

Mrs. Taylor will pay you more than Mrs. Green. Do you stay with your first promise or do you call Mrs. Green and offer an excuse about not being able to tend for her?

6. You are on your way to play ball with the boys and are already late. Down the block you see Mrs. Kelly carrying a heavy bag of groceries. You have always tried to help Mrs. Kelly whenever you could. Do you offer to help her carry the groceries, knowing the boys will go on without you, or do you hurry and turn the corner before she sees you?

7. Your mother has told you that even though she will not be home after school you are to go directly home to practice your piano lesson. A popular girl in your class—one you have long wished would be your friend—has invited you to come to her house after school to see her doll collection. You know this will delay your getting home half an hour, but since your mother will not be there anyway, she will never know. What would you do?

8. As you go to bed at night you think back over the day's activities. You think of four things you have done which were truly good, but one thing that you did that was wrong. Do you go to bed content, feeling that the good you did cancels the bad?

(This quiz could be adapted to a question box or a buzz session—see page 32.)

Another type of quiz is the true or false quiz, such as the following one on the Book of Mormon. This is effectively used at the beginning of a lesson to show children what they need to understand better, or it can be used as a review at the conclusion of a lesson.

Book of Mormon Quiz
(true or false)

1. .... Lehi and his family leave Jerusalem and go into the wilderness. (True.)
2. .... Nephi and Lemuel were obedient to their Father's commandments. (False—Nephi and Sam were the obedient sons.)
3. .... Nephi and his brothers returned to Jerusalem because they wanted to. (False—they returned because the Lord commanded it.)

4. .... Nephi and his brothers returned only once to Jerusalem. (False—they returned once for the family of Ishmael and once to obtain the brass plates of Laban.)

5. .... The Lord provided Lehi and the others with a ball of direction called the Liahona. (True.)

6. .... When the people were divided, the followers of Laman and Lemuel were called Lemuelites. (False—they were called Lamanites.)

7. .... Prophets among the people foretold the birth of Christ. (True.)

8. .... The people had no way of knowing when Christ was born in Bethlehem. (False—they were given signs at the time of his birth.)

9. .... Jesus Christ, after his resurrection, visited the Nephites and established his Church among them. (True.)

10. .... The Nephites did not accept the teachings of Christ. (False—they did accept them.)

11. .... Moroni, the father of Mormon, was the last writer of the Book of Mormon. (False—Moroni was the last writer, but he was not the father of Mormon—he was the son of Mormon.)

12. .... When Moroni first appeared to Joseph Smith, he gave him the gold plates. (False—Joseph had to wait three years before receiving the plates.)

13. .... Joseph Smith showed the gold plates to all his friends and neighbors. (False—only a few people saw the gold plates.)

14. .... When the Book of Mormon was published, everyone agreed that Joseph Smith was a prophet. (False—the persecution of Joseph became more intense after the publication of the Book of Mormon.)

15. .... The Book of Mormon was written by Joseph Smith. (False—it was translated, not written, by him.)

16. .... There were three and also eight witnesses to
the Book of Mormon. (True.)

Children love to dream and pretend. Make-believe can be
a source of inspiration to children by giving them goals and
images to live up to. A constructive "make believe" activity is
to have each child in your family act out what he would like
to be in the Church when he grows up.

What Do You Want to Be?

Perhaps a little three-year-old would like to be a chorister.
The child could dress up in mother's old dress, a pair of old
glasses, and high heels. She could use a music stand, book and
stick, and pretend to be leading music. It won't be too difficult
for the rest of the family to guess what she wants to be!

Maybe a four-year-old boy could dress in his Sunday suit,
Daddy's shoes and hat, and carry a Bible and Book of Mormon.
Of course, he wants to be a missionary.

A child just a little older might enjoy dressing up in her
mother's clothes and depict a Sunday School teacher by carrying a flannelboard and pictures.

Other suggestions for "What Do You Want To Be" are:
the ward organist, Relief Society president, scoutmaster, Sunday School superintendent or secretary, Junior Sunday School
coordinator, nursery class teacher, or Primary president.

Here is an example of an educational game that your family will enjoy. Even the littlest children know about Noah and
Joseph Smith.

Who Am I?

Guessing games are fun as well as instructive. Help your
children know more about great spiritual leaders by playing
"Who Am I?" Let the players choose outstanding people from
both ancient and modern times, and then offer a few clues that
will identify the person they are pretending to be. The player
guessing correctly becomes the next one to give clues. Here
are some examples:

1. I was the first man on earth, and I lived in the Garden of Eden.
    My wife's name was Eve.
    Who am I? (Adam)

2. I warned the people that they must repent or the Lord would destroy them. I built an ark and lived on it with my family and many animals during a great flood.
    Who am I? (Noah)

3. I lived in a tent on the desert and had many servants, camels, and sheep. My wife's name was Sarah and my son was Isaac.
    Who am I? (Abraham)

4. My father was Isaac and my grandfather was Abraham. The Lord changed my name to Israel.
    I was the father of twelve sons.
    Who am I? (Jacob)

5. My father gave me a coat of many colors.
    I was sold by my brothers to a caravan of merchants and was taken to Egypt. I became prime minister of Egypt and later helped my family during the famine.
    Who am I? (Joseph)

6. To preserve my life, my mother hid me in a basket among the bulrushes where a princess found me.
    I later led my people out of captivity to a promised land.
    Who am I? (Moses)

7. When I was born, my mother promised my services to the Lord.
    I was taken to the temple to live with the Prophet Eli when still a child. I heard the Lord's voice when I was twelve years old. Who am I? (Samuel)

8. I herded sheep and was the youngest son of Jesse.
    I was chosen by the Lord through the Prophet Samuel to become king.
    I wrote many songs and played them on my harp.
    I also fought a giant named Goliath.
    Who am I? (David)

9. I am one of the two women who have a book named after them in the scriptures. The love I had for my mother-in-law,

Naomi, is one of the beautiful stories of the Old Testament.

I am also known as a gleaner.

Who am I? (Ruth)

10. Satan tried to make me unfaithful to the Lord by taking away my prosperity. I lost my wealth and was cursed with many painful boils, but I remained true to the Lord.

Who am I? (Job)

11. I interpreted King Nebuchadnezzar's dream.

At another time I was cast into a den of lions but was not injured.

Who am I? (Daniel)

12. My writings can be found in the Old Testament.

I was swallowed by a great fish and lived there for three days.

Who am I? (Jonah)

13. My mission was to prepare the way for Christ.

I preached among the people and baptized many.

I baptized the Savior.

Who am I? (John the Baptist)

14. I was an Apostle of Jesus Christ when he was here on the earth.

My occupation was fishing.

After the death of the Savior I became the head of the Church on earth.

As a resurrected being I appeared to Joseph Smith with James and John and gave him the Melchizedek Priesthood.

Who am I? (Peter)

15. I was known as "The Beloved" Apostle to Jesus Christ. The Savior, while on the cross, asked me to care for his mother.

I wrote several books in the New Testament including the Book of Revelation.

Who am I? (John)

16. I persecuted the Church during the time of Christ, but upon my conversion I devoted the rest of my life to preaching the gospel.

I traveled extensively throughout the Church.

Who am I? (Paul)

17. My father's name was Lehi and my mother Sariah.
    I lived in Jerusalem and then journeyed to the Promised
    Land.
    I kept records about my people on brass plates.
    Who am I? (Nephi)

18. I am the oldest son of Lehi.
    I rebelled against my father and the teachings of the Lord.
    Who am I? (Laman)

19. I was a great and beloved king in the Book of Mormon.
    I spoke to my people from a high tower shortly before my
    death.
    The main theme of my life and my talk was service
    to others.
    Who am I? (King Benjamin)

20. I was a great Lamanite prophet.
    I preached from the walls of the Nephite city Zarahemla.
    I prophesied about the birth and death of Christ.
    Who am I? (Samuel the Lamanite)

21. We are three chosen disciples of Jesus.
    We made a special request of the Savior to remain on the
    earth until he comes again.
    Who are we? (The three Nephites)

22. I was a great Nephite general and prophet.
    One of the standard works is called by my name.
    Who am I? (Mormon)

23. My father's name was Mormon.
    After he was killed, I completed the record he had been
    making of our people.
    I buried this record which was written on gold plates, in a
    hill.
    As a resurrected being I appeared to Joseph Smith.
    Who am I? (Moroni)

24. When just 14 years old I received a remarkable vision.
    I later established The Church of Jesus Christ of Latter-
    day Saints.
    I was killed by a mob when 38 years old.
    Who am I? (Joseph Smith)

25. I was the second President of the Church.
    I led the members of the Church across the plains to the

Salt Lake Valley. I am known as a great colonizer.
Who am I? (Brigham Young)

(You can develop a question on each of the church Presidents using information from the flip chart entitled "Presidents of the Church" pages 77 to 87.)

Follow the Dots

The following idea would be a good attention-getter as well as put the children in a pleasant mood for a lesson. Instead of saying "Tonight we are having a lesson on the Bible" or "Tonight we're going to talk about a home," think how much more interested the children will be if you say, "Here is a follow-the-dots puzzle. The first one to finish will be the first to know what we are going to talk about tonight." You can invent your own puzzles quite easily. Here are two very simple ones:

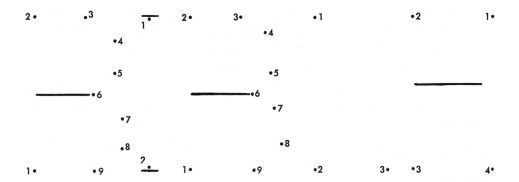

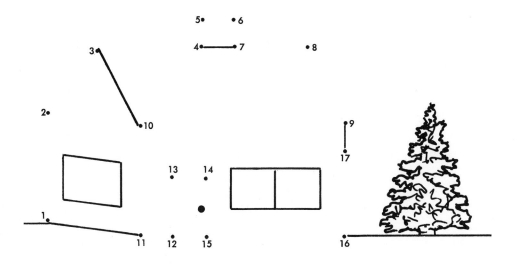

Work Sheets

Work sheets are another method of approach to a lesson. For example, the following work sheet might be used for a lesson on prayer. Make a copy for each family member, fold it in half so they can't see the bottom part of the paper, then tell them they are to make a very important decision. Only one of the roads will lead them to happiness and joy in the gospel— the other four to less desirable goals. But because of the inability to see and understand all the facts, they need help in making their decisions. Then let them choose one road to follow, and they can see just where they might end without help in their decisions. A lesson on the value of prayer could then follow.

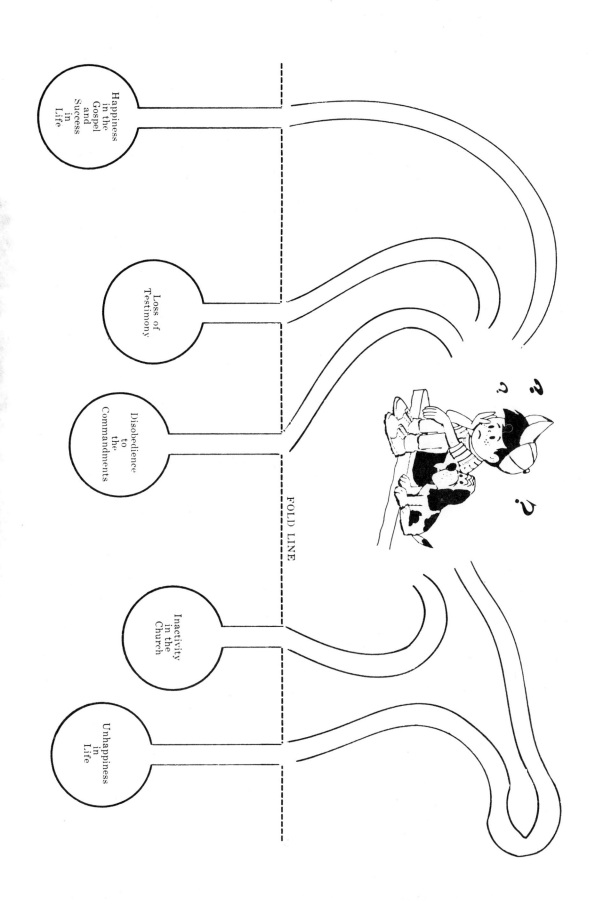

Another work sheet idea that may help solve a common family problem is this one. First hand each family member a duplicate of the map without saying anything about it. They naturally will begin to ask, "What's this for" or "What are we supposed to do with this." Point out that without instructions we seldom know what we are supposed to do. Next give each person the incomplete instructions and tell them to follow them. Naturally they will be unable to reach their destination. Finally provide them with complete and accurate instructions. Then they should easily be able to reach their goal. The point should then be clear—we must listen carefully and then follow accurately the instructions we are given. So often we don't hear at all or only half listen. Learning to follow instructions is an important part of all phases of life.

Incomplete Directions:
Begin at home on corner of 2nd South and 2nd East.
Proceed west on 2nd South two blocks.
Turn that direction and go to
Turn   and go a certain number of blocks to 2nd East.
Go north   blocks and then turn left.
Proceed two blocks in a direction. Turn   one block.
Turn   two blocks.
Turn left and proceed to   street corner.
Get out of car and walk to structure on corner.

Complete Directions:
Begin at home on corner of 2nd South and 2nd East.
Proceed west on 2nd South two blocks.
Turn north and go to 1st South.
Turn east and go two blocks to 2nd East.
Go north one block and then turn west.
Proceed two blocks west. Turn south one block.
Turn east one block.
Turn north and proceed to next street corner.
Turn west one more block.
Get out of car and walk to structure on corner.

Map

TEMPLE SQUARE	Hotel Utah Church Offices Beehive House	Apartments	Second East

South Temple

	Z C M I C M I Telephone Bank Company	Planetarium Fire Station	

First South

	Genealogy Library Bank	Federal Gas Building Company	

Main Street · State Street

Second South

			☐ Home

N

W —⊕— E

S

Crossword puzzles are helpful in teaching children important gospel terminology as well as the spelling of important words. Here are two crossword puzzles your family will enjoy:

Church History — Crossword Puzzle

ACROSS

1. The first President and Prophet of the Church was Joseph ....

4. The Saints who came across the plains in covered wagons were called ....

8. The Book of Mormon was .... by Joseph Smith.

12. Joseph Smith received many .... to help him establish the Church.

13. The Saints built a beautiful city in Illinois called ....

15. The best way to travel in those days was by covered ....

17. The pioneers knew their journey would not be ....

19. To receive the blessings of the Lord, all members of his Church must .... what he asks them to.

20. First the Aaronic, ... the Melchizedek Priesthood was restored.

21. The Book of Mormon is a second .... for Jesus Christ.

DOWN

2. Knowledge of the gold plates was brought to Joseph Smith by the Angel ....

3. "Come, Come, Ye Saints" became a familiar .... as the pioneers crossed the plains.

4. The history of the ancient inhabitants of America was engraved on golden ....

5. Most of the covered wagons were pulled by ....

6. The early members of the Church often did not have enough to ....

7. Joseph Smith, when 14 years old, was visited by God the Father and his .... Jesus Christ.

9. The second President of the Church was Brigham ....

10. The first pioneers arrived in Salt Lake Valley on .... 24, 1847.
11. A Latter-day Saint is commonly called a ....
14. The Lord commanded the Saints to establish their home in the ....
16. While driving a team of oxen, familiar expressions were ....! and Haw!
18. Emma Smith was known in church history because .... was the Prophet's wife.

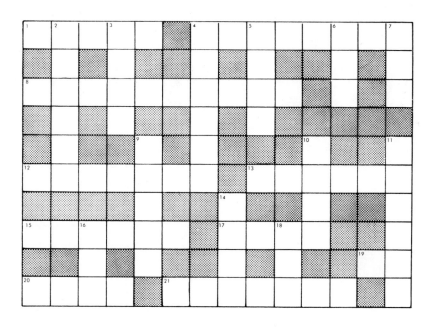

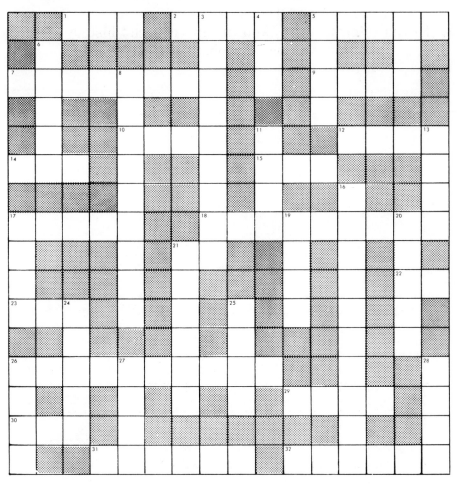

(Answers on page 144)

Baptism — Crossword Puzzle

ACROSS

1. When you are confirmed, men will .... their hands upon your head.

2. and 5.   They will give you the gift of the ....

7. Before you can be confirmed a member of the Church you must be ....

9. The place where we are baptized is called a baptismal ....

10. Before you are baptized you should know the basic principles of the gospel and understand what they .... to you.

12. Before being baptized, a short meeting will be held in which someone will .... to you about the important thing you are doing.

14. Even though you will still make some mistakes, you must .... constantly to do what you know is right after you have been baptized.

15. The gift of the Holy Ghost is more precious than anything else you will ever ....

17. When you are baptized, you will .... completely in white clothing to indicate purity.

18. To become a member of the Church, you are first baptized and then ....

21. On the days you are baptized and confirmed, ... your parents, are very proud of you.

22. One of the things you must do to prepare yourself for baptism is to .... to your church meetings faithfully.

23. When Christ was baptized, the people .... the Holy Ghost descend upon him like a dove.

26. You will be baptized and confirmed by men who hold the ....

29. In fast meeting you will probably want to .... the songs with more enthusiasm than before because of the happiness that should be within your heart.

30. The Lord says that eight years old is the .... of accountability.

31. After being baptized and confirmed, you will be a .... of The Church of Jesus Christ of Latter-day Saints.

32. Before being baptized, you will be interviewed by the .... of your ward.

DOWN

3. Faith is a principle of the gospel that leads to the .... of baptism.

4. This event is more important to .... than to anybody else.

6. We know we must be baptized with .... just as Christ was.

8. Heavenly Father has told us we must be baptized by ....

11. The person that baptized Christ was named .... the Baptist.

13. You must promise the Lord to try and be the .... of person he would like you to be.

16. The Holy Ghost can help you only if you listen carefully to the .... you will receive during your lifetime.

19. You will be confirmed in a meeting called .... meeting.

20. You must be .... years old before you can be baptized.

21. You must also be .... to be baptized which means you must be doing the things the Lord has asked you to do.

24. The clothes you wear will be .... in color.

25. It is very important that you .... how important this occasion is to you.

26. It is important for you to .... often to ask for help in making decisions, and to thank the Lord for your many blessings.

27. After you have been baptized, your life will never be quite the ...., for you are now old enough to accept responsibility for the things you do.

28. For this reason it is very important that you .... the Lord's commandments.

There are many other games your family would enjoy. You might like to play Twenty Questions using a gospel subject. Or perhaps a gospel spelling bee would be helpful in which words are spelled (and defined, if you would like). Words you might use are patriarchal, Priesthood, Melchizedek, Aaronic, dispensation, and millennium.

Games which have been developed by members of the Church and sold through bookstores offer another excellent learning medium.

(For another "Sugar 'n Spice" idea, refer to chalkboard suggestions, pages 51-96, in *Teaching with New Techniques* by Charles R. Hobbs, published by Deseret Book Company.)

(The story on page 13, "A Story of Three Families," could easily be adapted as a chalk talk.)

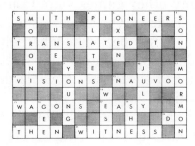

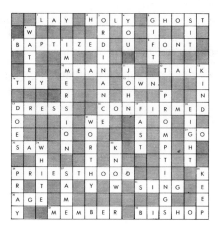

Index